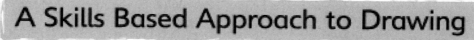
A Skills Based Approach to Drawing

Drawing
is a Class Act

Years 5–6

Meg Fabian

Brilliant Publications

'In learning to draw (unlike
learning to write) you learn to look.'
'Then you teach yourself to see and
to feel what you see.'
*David Hockney
from the forward to Draw:
How to Master the Art by
Jeffrey Camp*

Acknowledgements

I would like to thank:

Andrew Riley, Primary Phase Adviser and erstwhile Headteacher at two of the primary schools where I have taught art, for his help, advice, encouragement and inspiration not only in the initial stages of this book but also during all the time we worked together.

Dr Aubrey Wilson for his sterling advice and support.

Chris Wightman and Phil Creek, the Devon Curriculum Services Art Advisers, for all the art courses they have run, when I have turned up exhausted and jaded and left enthused and full of ideas.

I would also like to thank the following primary schools for their permission to include in the publication examples of work by children in their schools. This work has been done over a number of years. Wherever work is named, permission was sought for inclusion.

Primary schools
Berrynarbor
Burrington
Chawleigh
Clovelly
East Worlington
Filleigh
Winkleigh
Witheridge

Individual pupils
Ahmed Razak
Alexandra Mills
Becky Jewel
Bethan Vanstone
Bob Rush
Callum Clark
Callum Gregory
Charlotte Green
Daisy Perham
Danny Hudson
Eliza Burt
Felicity Cook
George Porter
Harmony Wilton
Harriet Gregory
Heidi Green
Holly Peacock
Hope Alexander
Jack Perham
Jacob Prangell
Jade Tanton
Jessica Pearson
Jordan Clark
Leanna Lyons-Martin
Lemar Bradford
Melissa Peddar
Michael McCormack
Michael Grimshire
Oliver Vanstone
Poppy Bell
Rebecca Lumb
Sam Jeffrey
Sarah Vanstone
Stephen Angold
Stephen Grimshire
Thomas Ellis
Victoria Braund
Victoria Rawlings
Zac Anderson
Zoe Elder

The publishers and author would like to thank the following for permission to reproduce artwork in this book (page nos. given in brackets):

Addison Gallery of Art, Andover, MA, USA (162); Design and Artists Copyright Society (DACS) (159 bottom right, 163, 167, 173 left); Kroller-Muller Museum, Otterlo (25, 157); Kunsthistorisches Museum, Vienna (85); Museum of Amsterdam (23, 154 and 174); Museum of Modern Art, New York (167); Tate, London 2005 (24, 155, 156, 158, 159, 161, 163, 173, 176), Victoria and Albert Museum, London (170); Sarah Wimperis (160); Windsor Castle (18 and 153)

The publishers apologise if they have inadvertently miscredited anyone for any of the works of art used in this book. We will correct any mistakes pointed out to us as soon as feasible.

Brilliant Publications, Unit 10, Sparrow Hall Farm, Edlesborough, Dunstable, Bedfordshire LU6 2ES
Tel: 01525 222292
Fax: 01525 222720
e-mail: info@brilliantpublications.co.uk
website: www.brilliantpublications.co.uk
The name Brilliant Publications and the logo are registered trademarks.

Written by Meg Fabian
Illustrations supplied by class pupils (see list above)
Front cover design by Lynda Murray
Cover illustrations by Hope Alexander, Lemar Bradford, Hannah Brown, Martyn Dallyn, Holly Peacock, Jack Perham and Bethan Vanstone

Foreword

Many of the examples in this book have been developed through collaborative work across a number of small primary schools in Devon. The schools worked with Meg Fabian over a period of two years. This collaborative work, involving a specialist with a passion for her subject, was instrumental in raising children's standards and confidence in drawing. Teachers also benefited from gaining knowledge and skills to improve their own understanding and teaching of drawing.

It became clear during the collaborative work that teachers needed the guidance and encouragement of a subject specialist: this is what this book provides for all teachers. By clearly setting out the development of drawing skills from the beginning, offering guidance on progression in learning and providing ideas to support classroom activities, this book is exactly what busy primary teachers need.

The schools involved in this innovative collaborative work believed in the importance of raising standards in art and the impact this has on the promotion of high standards in other subjects of the curriculum and, importantly, in children's self-esteem and confidence. The schools reflected this belief in practice and dedicated a higher proportion of time to the teaching of art. They also recognized that, to achieve high standards in art, the class teacher may need support in identifying the developmental stages of drawing.

This is where this book will be an invaluable resource.

David Chaplin
Lead Adviser
Devon Curriculum Services

Year 6 child's fine line pen drawing

Contents

	Page
Acknowledgements	2
Forward	3
A skills-based approach to drawing	7
How the skills-based approach works	7
What the book covers	8
About drawing	8–9
About looking	9
Moving on in drawing, leaving schema behind	10–11
Range of media	12–13
Sketchbooks	14–15
Erasers and rulers	16

	Type of lesson	Time needed	Page no(s).
Line			**17–44**
Rationale			18
Drawing light lines			18–19
About this chapter			19
Making different types of line in pencil	**Key skill**	**30 min.**	**20**
Different lines in pencil	Using skill	30–45 min.	21
Expectations after covering key skill			22
Looking at line in works of art 1	Try this idea!	20 min.	23
Looking at line in works of art 2	Try this idea!	20 min.	24
Looking at line in words of art 3	Try this idea!	20 min.	25
Pens			26
Making different lines with fine, medium and broad line pens	Skill	15 min.	27
Fine, medium and broad line pens	Using skill	30 min.	28
Fine line pens	Using skill	30 min.	29
Medium line pens	Using skill	20 min.	30
Broad line pens	Using skill	20 min.	31
Drawing lines with different character	Skill	20 min.	32–33

	Type of lesson	Time needed	Page no(s).
Line (continued)			
Using line to create tone	Skill	30 min.	34
Single- and cross-hatching	Using skill	30 min.	35
Illusions with line	Try this idea!	30 min.	36–37
Pens with nibs 1	Skill	15 min.	38
Pens with nibs 2	Using skill	30–45 min.	39
Making different lines with charcoal	Skill	10 min.	40
Drawing with charcoal	Using skill	30 min.	41
Scraper technique 1	Skill	1 hour	42–43
Scraper technique 2	Using skill	1 hour	44

	Type of lesson	Time needed	Page no(s).
Tone			**45–56**
Rationale			46
What is tone?			46
About this chapter			47
Making different tones in pencil	**Key skill**	**30–40 min.**	**48–49**
Using tone to shade three-dimensional shapes	Using skill	30 min.	50–51
Making different tones in pencil 1	Using skill	15 min.	52
Making different tones in pencil 2	Using skill	30–40 min.	53
Making different tones with charcoal	Skill	15–20 min.	54–55
Creating tone with charcoal	Using skill	30–45 min.	56

	Type of lesson	Time needed	Page no(s).
Texture			**57–60**
Rationale			58
About this chapter			58
Drawing different textures	**Key skill**	**30 min.**	**59**
Drawing textures	Using skill	30 min.	60
Pattern			**61–72**
Rationale			62
What is pattern?			62–63
About this chapter			63
Making patterns with lines and shapes 1	**Key skill**	**30 min.**	**64–65**
Making patterns with lines and shapes 2	**Key skill**	**30–40 min.**	**66–67**
Using line patterns in a doodle	Using skill	15 min.	68–69
Collecting patterns from nature	Try this idea!	30 min.	70
Using patterns and shapes from nature to create designs	Try this idea!	45 min.	71
Collecting patterns from different cultures or times	Try this idea!	30–40 min.	72
Looking			**73–112**
Why looking skills are so important			74
Rationale			74
Helping children to look with new eyes			75
About this chapter			76
List of possible subjects for drawing or discussion			77
Focusing looking through talking	**Key skill**	**20 min.**	**78–79**
Talking about the subject before drawing	Using skill	45 min.	80–81

	Type of lesson	Time needed	Page no(s).
Looking (continued)			
Using focusing devices	Skill	45 min.	82–83
Using viewfinders to look for detail and content	Using skill	30–40 min.	84–85
Looking for shape and form	Skill	15 min.	86–87
Recognizing and drawing right angles and parallel lines	Skill	30 min.	88–89
Drawing geometric shapes	Skill	30–45 min.	90
Drawing objects by looking for shapes	Using skill	30–45 min.	91
Sighting	Skill	15 min.	92
Drawing using sighting	Using skill	35–40 min.	93
Learning to see relationships between line and shape	Skill	20 min.	94–95
Seeing relationships between line and shape when drawing	Using skill	30–40 min.	96–97
How drawing is affected by the two halves of the brain			98–99
How the left side of the brain causes problems	Try this idea!	15-20 min.	100–101
Seeing negative shapes	Skill	15 min.	102
Seeing and drawing negative shapes	Using skill	45 min.	103
Slowing down the speed of looking	Skill	20–30 min.	104–105
Looking and drawing very slowly	Using skill	20 min.	106–107
Looking, holding, drawing a line	Skill	20 min.	108–109
Drawing upside down	Try this idea!	30 min.	110–111
Looking strategies children could use when drawing			112
Self-assessment of looking strategies			112

	Type of lesson	Time needed	Page no(s).
Figures and faces			**113–132**
Rationale			114
Basic rules			114–115
About this chapter			115
Drawing the whole body	**Key skill**	**45 min.**	**116–117**
Drawing different poses	**Key skill**	**40 min.**	**118**
Contour figure drawing	Skill	30 min.	119
Gesture figure drawing	Skill	30 min.	120
Figure drawing from memory	Skill	30 min.	121
Drawing heads and position of features	Skill	30 min.	122–123
Drawing eyes	Skill	30 min.	124–125
Drawing mouths and noses	Skill	30 min.	126–127
Drawing faces	Using skill	45–60 min.	128–129
Drawing faces in profile	Using skill	45–50 min.	130–131
Detailed whole-body portrait	Using skill	50–60 min.	132

Chalk and charcoal			**133–141**
Rationale			134
Media knowledge			134–135
Tips and techniques			136
About this chapter			137
Making different marks in chalk and charcoal	**Key skill**	**15–20 min.**	**138–139**
Drawing with chalk and charcoal	Using skill	30–45 min.	140–141

	Type of lesson	Time needed	Page no(s).
Evaluation and assessment			**142–149**
Assessment			143–144
Using success criteria to evaluate children's work			144
Self-evaluation			145–146
Peer evaluation			147
Reporting and tracking progress			148
Recording coverage of work			148
Reports			149
Glossary			150
Bibliography			151
Useful websites			152
Resource sheets			153–181

A skills-based approach to drawing

The aim of this book is to support non-specialist art teachers working in primary schools. It is intended for teachers who say, *'I want to help my children get better at drawing but I don't know how,'* and to help teachers respond confidently to all those children who say, *'I'm rubbish at drawing.'*

This book is designed to be easily accessible. It is intended that teachers can glance at a page, read the title, look at the example of pupils' work and know what to do without reading all the text. Teachers wanting further information can read the page.

Each lesson plan includes:
- ☐ Lesson title indicating the skill or technique being covered
- ☐ Logo indicating the type of lesson:

- ☐ Time needed to complete the lesson
- ☐ Resources
- ☐ Links to National Curriculum programmes of study
- ☐ Introduction to pupils
- ☐ Practical activity
- ☐ Examples of pupils' work.

Many lessons also include:
- ☐ Background information necessary to deliver the lesson
- ☐ Examples of works of art that illustrate the use of the skills being taught.

Some lessons include:
- ☐ A photocopiable worksheet
- ☐ Possible pitfalls.

How the skills-based approach works

The principle of this book is that the skills and techniques covered should be used for a purpose as soon as possible. It is important that children have the opportunity to use their skills in a drawing context.

For this reason a 'Using skill' lesson follows each 'Skill' lesson throughout the book. For example, when children have learned the skills for using line with charcoal they can then use these skills to draw school buildings, windswept trees, etc. This also gives the teacher a clear focus for assessment.

The drawing subject could be linked to another appropriate topic, for example if the local environment is being studied in history or geography, then this is an excellent opportunity to apply the art skills to drawing landscape.

For some lessons it is recommended that teachers demonstrate or model basic techniques. This generally involves nothing more challenging than drawing light and dark lines using charcoal or drawing a cube on the board. Paper can be fixed to the board with Blu-tac® for demonstrating. Where paper is necessary for teacher modelling, it is mentioned in the resources list for that lesson.

Many of the skills exercises will result in a piece of work that is visually pleasing in its own right. Children will produce something they can be proud of. This factor has been deliberately built in. Very often, once the skill has been taught, the pieces of work can be adapted or mounted to produce a stunning piece of artwork that can be displayed to great effect. There are some good examples of this in the 'Illusions with line' lesson (see pages 36–37). If it makes the children feel *'Wow, I did that'*, it will increase their confidence, their self-esteem and their willingness to take the next step.

The skills-based approach doesn't inhibit creativity; it helps children to know how to create certain effects. If they have increased control and understanding of the different media, they will be able to experiment with more confidence and be empowered to express themselves.

What the book covers

This book covers all the National Curriculum programmes of study related to drawing. The programmes of study are listed for each lesson.

The book has chapters on line, tone, texture, pattern, looking, figures and faces, and chalk and charcoal. The contents pages clearly set out the lessons for each chapter, giving the type of lesson and approximate time needed for each. There is also a chapter on evaluation and assessment.

The book:
- ☐ Clearly sets out the progression of skills
- ☐ Has lessons plans for upper juniors which can be adapted easily for small schools with mixed age ranges, or single-age classes where there is a wide range of ability
- ☐ Has examples of pupils' artwork showing the skills at each stage
- ☐ Gives examples of how the skills can be applied (children are more motivated when they can see clearly how the skill can be used)
- ☐ Has responses to works of art integrated into each unit
- ☐ Has photocopiable reproductions of works of art and other photocopiable resources (all of which are to be found at the back of the book).

It is not expected that all the lessons will be delivered. Teachers can teach one, some, or most of the lessons. However, if there is very limited time, then it is suggested that just the key skill lessons are taught.

These lessons are marked with this symbol. The key skill lessons appear in bold on the contents pages.

Other books in the series

This book is one of a series of three. The other books in the series cover Key Stage 1 and lower Key Stage 2.

Years 1–2   ISBN 1 903853 60 5 (978-1-903853-60-3)
Years 3–4   ISBN 1 903853 61 3 (978-1-903853-61-0)

About drawing

Dictionary derivation of 'to draw':
- ☐ Old High German   Tragen
- ☐ Old High Norse   Draga
- ☐ Old High Goth   Gadragon
- ☐ Old English   Dragon

The various ways we use the word 'drawing' are fascinating, at once connected, and yet different:
- ☐ To draw out
- ☐ To be drawn along
- ☐ To be drawn into
- ☐ To draw alongside
- ☐ To draw from experience
- ☐ To draw closer …

'It is the *draw closer* that is the most interesting. When I am drawing, I become totally involved, I concentrate intensely, become more closely involved with what I am drawing. There comes a point when I am almost at one with my subject, I feel all my senses are engaged. I miss nothing.'
Meg Fabian, the author

So many adults feel that they cannot draw; this is perhaps because they have never been taught to draw. Anyone can draw up to a certain level of competence.

> 'Most adults in the Western world do not progress in art skills beyond the level of the development they reached at nine or ten. In most mental and physical activities individuals' skills change and develop as they grow to adulthood. The development of drawing skills, however, seems to halt unaccountably at an early age for most people. This could be because drawing is not a vital skill for survival in our culture, but reading and writing are.'
>
> *Betty Edwards, Drawing on the Right Side of the Brain*

Learning to draw is something that never stops. Children are surprised when they hear that artists go on learning and getting better all their lives, that they never consider they have stopped developing as artists.

Drawing is surrounded by mystique. It is commonly imagined that the few who can perform its magical rites have been invested with a divine gift – but actually anyone can learn to draw.

> 'From the age of six, I had a mania for drawing the form of things. At seventy-five I learned a little about the real structure of nature. At ninety I shall penetrate the mystery of things; at a hundred I shall have reached a marvellous stage; and when I am a hundred and ten, everything I do, be it a dot or a line, will be alive.'
>
> *Written at the age of 75 by Owakio Rojin, an old man mad about drawing (from Betty Edwards, Drawing on the Right Side of the Brain)*

There are many purposes for drawing, for example recording, expressing, communicating and analyzing.

This book is about exploring the media and elements.

About looking

The key to drawing is in the looking. For this reason a separate chapter is devoted to it.

Children find it hard to believe that as artists their eyes are more important than their hands. The skills covered in the Looking chapter will help them understand how and why this is true. They will be guided not only to look closely but to look with purpose and to develop different ways of looking.

> 'In developing children's ability to see and understand various visual situations you produce a storehouse of ideas that can be used in countless different ways.'
>
> *Ian Simpson, Drawing, Seeing and Observation*

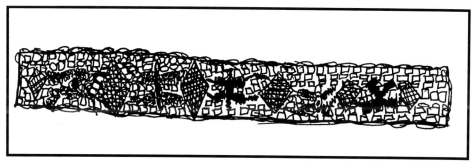

Year 5 child's drawing of a piece of lace

9

Moving on in drawing, leaving schema behind

The most difficult task children have to overcome in drawing is that they live in a three-dimensional world which they are trying to represent on a two-dimensional surface.

Schema

When they are younger, children solve this problem by drawing symbols or schema. Shapes rarely overlap each other and subject matter is surrounded by space. The bottom of the paper serves as the ground and most subjects are drawn facing the viewer. A sun is drawn as a quarter circle in one upper corner.

Heads are often round and too big, the mouth is a line and necks are forgotten, shoulders are too narrow, arms too short and feet point the same way.

Example of Year 5–6 schema

Example of Year 5–6 schema

There is nothing wrong with schema as long as children don't get 'fixed' in the schematic stage and become unable to move on. Children often need to use schema to quickly create storyboards, to record ideas or to illustrate work from another curriculum area.

At Years 5 and 6 observational drawing is developed alongside narrative drawing as both have their place, just as notes or plans for written work exist alongside extended writing.

This next stage of children's drawing development is probably the hardest. Children need to move away from their comfortable schema, look longer and harder and think more carefully before they draw. The spontaneity in drawing seems to have gone. This is a crucial stage in drawing in which children need strategies to help them succeed. Some children will want to give up, they can become frustrated when their drawings don't 'go right'; their drawings seem to lack the charm of younger children's but are not yet as competent as they would like. They have an idea of how they think their drawings should look, but they feel their ability falls way below their aspirations.

It is a great shame that older primary pupils feel so strongly that the only 'good' drawing is one that looks realistic. It is difficult for them to understand that expressive drawing is equally valid, that their drawings have character and vividness that is much admired by adult artists. This is when many children first gain the notion that they are 'no good at art'. This idea often stays with them through life. This is tragic.

If they are given structured support and some tips and techniques to help them through this stage, they will quickly realize that they can make good progress and achieve results that will satisfy and encourage them. Years 5 and 6 children are the harshest critics of their own artwork.

Being able to draw well brings considerable peer approval and gives increased confidence to young artists, but they need to understand that it will involve having a serious attitude, applying themselves and perseverance. However, it will not be easy.

Sarah Vanstone, Year 6

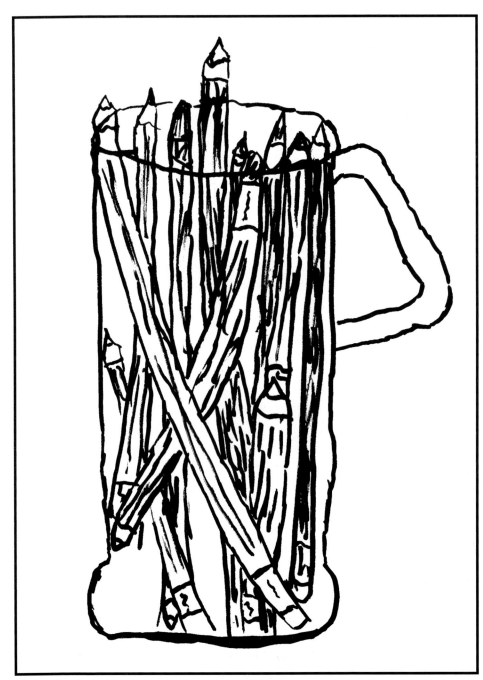

Victoria Rawlings, Year 6

Range of media

To deliver the lessons in this book you will need (absolute basics are in bold):

❑ One set of drawing pencils H to 8B for display
❑ B, **2B** and 4B **pencils**
❑ **Fine line pens (tip size 0.4 mm)**
❑ Permanent pens, medium tip
❑ Permanent pens, broad tip (round tips are more manageable than chisel)
❑ Erasers
❑ **Charcoal, medium thickness**
❑ **White chalk** or white chalky pastel
❑ **Fixative** (see Glossary)
❑ **Oil pastels**
❑ Brusho (powdered watercolour)
❑ Coloured pencils, art quality
❑ Conté crayons (soft pastels)
❑ Pens with nibs and ink
❑ Sketchbooks (A4)
❑ Viewfinders (see Glossary and page 82)
❑ Magnifying glasses
❑ Mirrors (plastic)
❑ Cartridge paper (see Glossary)

Starting-out kit:

Tip: buy good-quality media, topping up when you can. Gradually extend range a little at a time.

- ❏ B and 4B pencils (add 2B when you can)
- ❏ Fine line pens (tip size 0.4 mm), water-based
- ❏ Permanent pens, broad tip (add medium tip when you can)
- ❏ Charcoal, medium thickness
- ❏ Fixative
- ❏ Oil pastels (extend range of colours later)
- ❏ Art pastels (chalky)
- ❏ Art quality coloured pencils. (These are expensive so could be left until budget allows. The water colour pencils are the most versatile as they can be used in two ways: as coloured pencils and as a form of water colours.)
- ❏ Sketchbooks with cartridge paper pages
- ❏ Viewfinders made from cut black sugar paper (replace with card or corrugated plastic when you can)

> 'Drawing is the discipline by which I constantly rediscover the world. I have learned that what I have never drawn I have never seen, and when I start drawing an ordinary thing, I realize how extraordinary it is, sheer miracle.'
> Frederick Frank, The Zen of Seeing

> 'For me drawing is a kind of thinking, but it is also about the medium.'
> Antony Gormley, sculptor of The Angel of the North (from his book, Drawing)

A well-resourced art cupboard could have:

- ❏ H, B, 2B, 4B, 6B pencils
- ❏ Fine line pens (tip size 0.3 mm and 0.4 mm), water-based
- ❏ Fine (tip size 0.4 mm), medium and broad permanent pens
- ❏ Charcoal, thick and thin
- ❏ Fixative
- ❏ Oil pastels, 25 colours, bright and subtle, extra white and black
- ❏ Art pastels, good range of colours, including landscape colours
- ❏ Conté crayons (soft pastels), black, white, earth colours, sepia, burned sienna, etc.
- ❏ Pens (with nibs) and drawing inks, including white
- ❏ Good-quality crayons, some sets in people colours
- ❏ Art quality coloured pencils, landscape and portrait sets
- ❏ Water colour pencils
- ❏ Graphite
- ❏ Metallic crayons
- ❏ Metallic pens – fine and broad
- ❏ Sketchbooks with cartridge paper pages
- ❏ Clipboards for outside drawing
- ❏ Black plastic viewfinders
- ❏ Magnifying glasses with flexible necks that clamp onto desk
- ❏ Lamps with flexible necks
- ❏ Collection of reproductions of works of art, filed according to topic or subject, or QCA art documents
- ❏ Collection of CD-Roms featuring works of art for use on computer and white boards
- ❏ Collection of artefacts for drawing (see list on page 77)

Sketchbooks

> 'Drawing sketches is like planting seeds in order to get pictures later.'
> Van Gogh, in a letter to his brother Theo
> (from The Letters)

Most artists use a sketchbook. It is a vital part of their equipment used to collect visual information and to record ideas and feelings. On his death Picasso left 178 sketchbooks, containing a huge variety of ideas recorded over a period of 60 years. A page from one of Vincent van Gogh's sketchbooks appears on page 174.

It is a good idea for children to see artists' sketchbooks and to hear how they use them. This could be part of a school visit by a practising artist. If this is not possible, members of a local art group would probably be willing to visit the school and allow the children to see their sketchbooks and answer children's questions about how they are used.

Throughout this book it is suggested that children do the work outlined in each lesson directly in their sketchbooks. Sketchbooks are listed in the resources list for most lessons. When it is not possible to work directly in the sketchbooks (for example, in the Chalk and charcoal chapter the drawings are executed on mid-tone sugar paper), the drawings could be stuck into the sketchbooks later.

A sketchbook is a wonderful record of a child's development as a young artist. Being able to look back at their work and see their progression raises children's self-esteem.

Teachers can write comments in sketchbooks just as they would in other subject books. Comments should be specific, for example: *'I like the way you have used different kinds of lines in this drawing,'* or *'I can tell that you were looking very carefully when you drew this.'*

Sketchbooks should be started in Key Stage 1, and carry on through the school. They should be at least A4 and of reasonable quality paper. Slightly bigger than A4 is ideal, as A4 paper can be stuck in without any overlaps. Work may often be done on loose paper and stuck in later, perhaps because the artwork is going to be displayed or work has been done on different types or colours of paper.

The sketchbook paper needs to be thick enough to take paint, as the sketchbooks should be used across the whole art curriculum. The paper should have slight texture, as very smooth paper is not ideal for pencil.

The covers should be stiff enough for the children to lean on when drawing outside. Hard-backed sketchbooks are excellent but they are expensive and heavy.

> 'A day passed without drawing is a day wasted.'
> Antony Gormley, sculptor of
> The Angel of the North
> (from his book, Drawing)

Sketchbooks can be used for different purposes:

❒ Collecting visual information
❒ Capturing an image
❒ Planning
❒ Trying out new skills
❒ Experimenting with media
❒ Visual storytelling
❒ Note-taking
❒ Designing
❒ Describing
❒ Storing ideas
❒ Recording research
❒ Recording investigations
❒ Recording responses
❒ Recording trips and visits
❒ Recording a visual diary

Sketchbooks are:

❒ A record of achievement
❒ A record of development

They can be used for assessment:

❒ Self-evaluation
❒ For reporting to parents
❒ As evidence

Sketchbooks are a source of inspiration.

Sarah Vanstone, Year 5 (page from sketchbook)

Erasers and rulers

Rulers

For most drawing, children do not need rulers. Lines drawn with rulers tend to be similar so the resulting drawings are often without life and character. If pupils become dependent on rulers, they miss the opportunity to develop their ability to draw straight lines.

Erasers

Erasers create far worse problems. Although erasers may be used when areas of dark charcoal need to be lifted, to help create contrast and depth, the rest of the time they create more problems than they solve.

If children have used erasers in previous art classes there are usually cries of indignation when their use is banned. Tell them that erasers destroy the surface of the paper, and further drawing on that surface is not as effective. Repeated rubbings out tend to crease the paper and look messy and heavy lines never rub out cleanly and always leave a grubby patch.

Some children may rub out almost everything they do and end up with little to show for their efforts.

Most important of all is the fact that, if children think they can rub something out, they tend not to approach the task with as much thought and observation as they should. They are more likely to launch into the drawing without those few extra moments of close looking and intense observation. They are inclined also to place the drawing on the paper without much forethought, secure in the knowledge that they can rub it out.

Whilst enthusiasm and a desire to get started are wonderful, they must be weighed up against the value of deep thought and close looking. A good balance of both is ideal.

If they cannot use a rubber, they will need to be that bit more thoughtful and observant, and this is what will help them to progress.

Explain all this to them as it helps if they understand that the ban on erasers is better for their own artistic development.

Year 5 child's doodle

Year 5 child's pen drawing with watercolour, inspired by Paul Klee

Line

Sam Jeffrey, Year 5

George Porter, Year 5

Rationale

Children's exploration of different lines in different media will enable them to use a range of lines in their own work. These activities will open their eyes to the huge variety of lines that they can use.

Children learning to draw lines soon discover that they are gaining control over a most powerful tool.

The simplest line suggests direction, divides space, and has length, width, tone and texture. It can enclose or define shape, and can suggest contour. It is with line that we create writing.

There are no limits to the possibilities of pencil. It is the most basic tool in the art of drawing and also one of the most versatile.

'Study for the Sfortza Monument' by Leonardo da Vinci, showing use of light lines (a larger, photocopiable version appears on page 153). Reproduced with permission from Windsor Castle

Drawing light lines

This is one of the areas that creates the most problems for children in drawing. The business of starting a drawing using light lines, so that you can alter them if necessary, is a very difficult one for children to grasp. This is not so vital in narrative drawing, but it becomes increasingly more important as children try to achieve a particular result.

Explaining to children why light lines are important

❏ Explain that when artists start out on a drawing they don't expect for one minute that they will get everything right first time. So they use light lines or marks that they can alter later if they need to.

❏ Children could be told: *'You have to start a drawing somewhere and you can't be sure you won't have to change something, so make it easier for yourself: start off with **light** lines. You can then put in the lines you think are better over the light lines.'*

❏ Show the children some examples of drawings by artists that show lines which have been drawn over, or next to, other lines. Drawings by Leonardo da Vinci are an excellent example. See Resource sheet 1 (page 153). Tell the children that he was a genius who worked as an artist for a very long time. He changed his drawings as he went along. The children will almost certainly want to change something too, so they should avoid using dark lines as it is much harder to change them.

❏ Say, for example, *'Leonardo didn't throw down his pencil when his drawings went wrong, saying, "I give up, I'm rubbish at drawing."'*
Try to take the pressure off them to feel they must get it right first time.

Different ways to help children use light lines

Try asking someone who can draw (it doesn't have to be an artist) to come in and draw in front of the children, thinking out loud as the drawing progresses, altering things as they go along. It's better if the person isn't too accomplished, as making the children feel daunted would be counterproductive.

It helps if children understand that it is the amount of pressure on the pencil that results in the darkness of the line. Try asking them to close their eyes, make a line on the paper and then guess how dark it will be. Then, ask them to make three more lines, each darker than the first, then three lighter ones. Look to see how well they have judged the darkness and lightness of the lines.

You could try referring to light lines as whispering or secret lines.

I talked to one newly qualified teacher whose class had produced some stunning drawings; you could clearly see light lines beneath the final ones. When I asked her how she had achieved this, she replied, *'Easy, I just gave them 2H pencils for the initial drawings, then 2B to improve and complete them.'* Then she added, *'If they do dark lines to begin with, I just tear the drawings up!'* Her first idea is worth a try.

About this chapter

Children's exploration of different lines in different media will enable them to use a range of lines in their own work. Children should be more able to achieve the effect they want. These activities will open their eyes to the huge variety of lines that they can use.

In this chapter children make their own line collections for future reference. They use their skills in a context. They experiment in a range of media, and investigate the use of line by other artists.

Where possible, model the skills: once the children have seen some examples, they should be able to continue and extend the work independently.

If you are short of time, do only the key skill lessons.

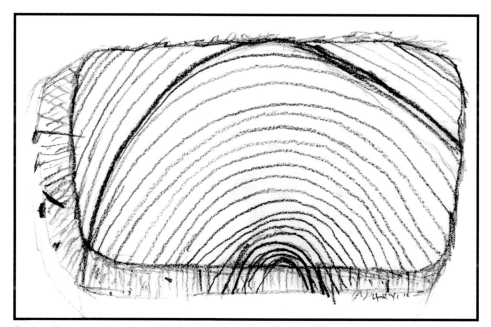

Bethan Vanstone, Year 6

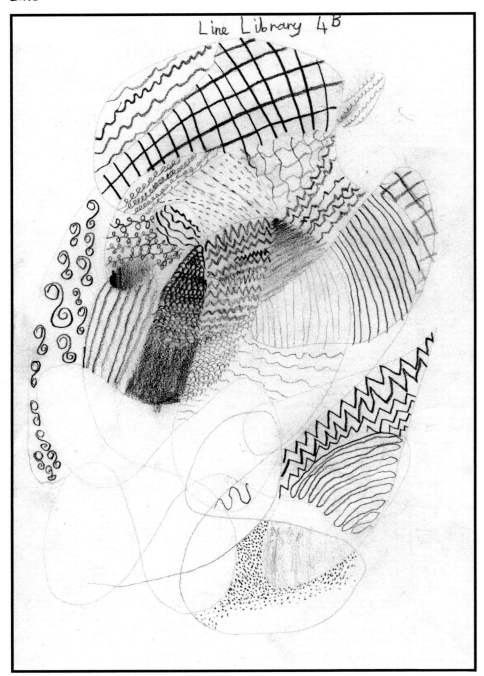

Year 5 child's collection of lines using 4B pencil

 KEY SKILL

Making different types of line in pencil

Time	Resources	National
30 min.	Sketchbooks	**Curriculum**
	B, 2B, 4B pencils (more if you have them)	2a, 4a
	One set of drawing pencils H to 8B	
	Large piece of white paper for teacher modelling	

Introduction

Introduce the subject by saying, *'One way to make your drawings more visually interesting, to give them more impact, more power, more sensitivity, is to use different types of lines. Lines can have character, mood, energy or delicacy. You will need to use the right kind of line to do the job you want.'*

Practical activity

❏ Show the selection of drawing pencils and demonstrate lines with the different pencils.

❏ Revise what the B and H stand for (black and hard). Model different kinds of lines: straight and curved, flowing and jagged, delicate and broken. Brainstorm a few more.

❏ Using one grade of pencil at a time, children make as many different types of line as they can.

❏ Explain that for each type of pencil they should draw light, medium and dark lines. Encourage them to use the side as well as the point of the pencil.

❏ Challenge children to make lines so delicate they are nearly invisible. Remind them that dots and dashes are lines too. They can be close together, far apart, light or dark.

❏ Ask children to think what lines could be used for – for example, dashes close together could be used for fur, hair or grass.

❏ Explain that they can use these collections of lines in the future, to remind themselves of just how many different types of lines there are. Tell them that you will be expecting to see lots of these lines used in their drawings.

USING SKILL

Different lines in pencil

Time	Resources	National
30–45 min.	B, 2B and 4B pencils Sketchbooks Artefacts such as flowers, wood (with grain showing) or topic-related artefacts (see list on page 77)	**Curriculum** 1a, 1c, 2b, 4a

Introduction
'Now you have drawn different kinds of lines, you are going to draw some objects that will give you a chance to use some of them. Don't forget to look back at your line collections in your sketchbooks.'

Practical activity
Once the children have chosen their subjects:
- ❏ Put out a selection of pencil grades. Children might like to work with only one, or to use them all.
- ❏ Tell them that you will be looking out for lots of different lines in their drawings.
- ❏ Explain that if they are drawing a subject that has hair or fur, the lines which represent the hair or fur should follow the shape of the form. This will help the drawings look more real and solid.

This activity can be used as an assessment activity (see assessment criteria on next page).

Background information
The children might like to select their own subjects for drawing from around the classroom. However, they may need some help in choosing subjects that will give them the opportunity to use their line drawing skills. They could draw each other or their own face in a mirror; outdoor settings are excellent, particularly if there is some grass or foliage. A list of possible subjects for drawing is on page 77.

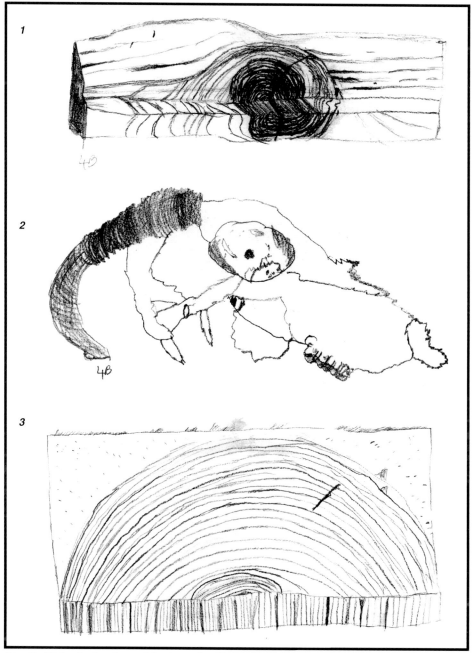

Year 5 children's drawings of 1: piece of split wood with the knot showing; 2: sheep's skull; 3: slice of wood with grain showing

Victoria Braund, Year 6 (pencil drawing of classroom plant)

Expectations after covering key skill

❐ All children will be able to draw a range of lines in three grades of pencil.

❐ Most will be able to use a number of these lines when drawing in context.

❐ Some children will be able to create different effects with different types of lines and grades of pencil, appropriate to the subject.

❐ A few children will use lines to dramatic effect, use delicate lines or lines showing character and sensitivity.

Success criteria as explained to children

❐ You **must** use a good variety of different lines.

❐ You **should** try to create different effects (relevant to subject) with different types of lines. You should use both the point and the side of the pencil.

❐ You **could** use lines to create dramatic effect, or delicate lines, where appropriate.

These criteria should really be drawn up with the children while the skill is being taught. Children can use the success criteria to make judgements about their own work, followed by teacher judgements. For further information on success criteria see page 144.

Looking at line in works of art 1

Time	Resources	National
20 min.	Sketchbooks	**Curriculum**
	Viewfinders (see Glossary)	4a, 4c
	B, 2B or 4B pencils	
	Resource sheet 2 (page 154)	

Introduction

'Today, you are going to look at a drawing done by Vincent van Gogh. It is remarkable how many different lines have been used in the one drawing. He uses lines for different purposes. For example, he creates the illusion of distance by using tiny lines.'

Practical activity

❐ Give out at least one copy of van Gogh's drawing (Resource sheet 2) and one viewfinder between two children.

❐ Ask children to slide the viewfinder over the picture and choose an area to look at closely.

❐ Keeping the viewfinder there, ask them to look at the variety of different kinds of lines they can see.

❐ Children copy these into their sketchbooks.

❐ This can be repeated with other areas of the picture.

'The Crau as seen from Mont Majour, 1888' by Vincent van Gogh (a larger, photocopiable version appears on page 154). Reproduced with permission from the Museum of Amsterdam

Background information
This lesson helps children to see where and how artists have used a variety of lines. They can discover for themselves how line can be used to create different effects, distance, texture, shadows, etc. Using viewfinders will help the children to focus on specific areas of a picture. It will help them to notice detail they might otherwise miss.

Lines found in above work of art using viewfinder

'Landscape Composition with Cliff to Left' by Alexander Cozens, with section omitted (a complete photocopiable version appears on page 155). Reproduced with permission from Tate, London 2005

Leanna Lyons-Martin, Year 5 (completed version of the above)

TRY THIS IDEA!

Looking at line in works of art 2

Time	Resources	National
20 min.	Resource sheets 3 and 4 (pages 155–156)	**Curriculum**
(10 min.	or other suitable line drawing reproductions;	4a, 5d
for each	mask part of drawing and photocopy it	
drawing)	Fine line pens or sharp B or 2B pencils	

Introduction
'The activity you are going to do today will help you to look even more closely at different types of lines in drawings.'

Practical activity
❑ Give each child a copy of one of the drawings (Resource sheets 3 and 4).
❑ Ask the children to fill in the missing areas using the same kind of lines the artist has used.
❑ Tell the children that if this is done very carefully, it should be nearly impossible to see where the space was.
❑ After this has been done children might like to see the original complete drawing and compare their lines against them.

Background information
This activity will help children to look closely not only at lines in a work of art, but also at composition and proportions. They will need to make logical predictions about the missing sections of drawings based on what they can see.

Looking at line in works of art 3
Questioning with a line focus

Time	Resources	National
20 min.	Resource sheets 5 and 6 (pages 157–158)	Curriculum 4a, 5d

Introduction
'When you have looked closely at these drawings and talked about them with the person next to you, I am going to ask you some questions about how line has been used.'

Practical activity
❐ Give each pair of children one of the drawings by van Gogh (Resource sheets 5 and 6).
❐ Children look at and discuss the drawings with a partner. Go over the questions you are going to ask. You could write them up on the board, or give the children a photocopy of them to read as they look at the pictures. It will help to focus their looking.
❐ The questions will vary according to the artwork used. Here are some examples relating to van Gogh's 'Head of a Woman' (the answers are given in italics, where appropriate):
 * How has the artist created shadow and darker areas?
   By using single- or cross-hatching (see page 34 and Glossary) or by using darker lines close together. Children might say by shading.
 * What medium do you think the artist has used?
 * Would charcoal have been a good medium for this subject?
 * Why do you think that?
 * Can you spot any dots or broken lines? Are dashes a regular distance apart?
 * Are there many straight lines? Why do you think that is?

'Head of a Woman' by Vincent van Gogh. Reproduced with permission from the Kroller-Muller Museum, Otterlo

Year 6 child's doodle

Pens

Once children have experimented with line in a range of media, it is interesting for them to experiment further with the use of contrasting widths of line.

Working in pen helps children create confident drawings. There is no possibility of rubbing out, and little opportunity to change lines. After some thought, they just have to launch into the drawing, knowing that what they put down will have to stay.

Fine line pens are very useful for crisp, delicate or detailed drawings. 0.4 mm is probably the finest tip appropriate to this age group.

Medium tip pens range from the average felt tip up to about 0.8 mm.

Broad pens could be anything from 1.6 mm upwards. Round tips are more manageable than chisel tips as children tend to forget which way to angle the point. Broad chisel/wedge tips give two possible widths of line with the same pen, according to which side of the tip is used. The usual widths are 2 mm and 5 mm. Broad pens are excellent for large-scale or group work. They are also good for creating borders for large-scale pictures.

Permanent pens are extremely useful, as paint or inks can be added to the drawings without the ink running. It is difficult to buy permanent fine pens, so the drawings can be photocopied and then paint added. Berol® make a double-ended permanent pen which has tips of two different thicknesses.

Lovely effects can be achieved by wetting water-based pen drawings with a damp fine brush. The black line goes a soft dark brown, and the lines blur a little. If the tip of a wet brush is touched against the lines the ink can be spread across a small area. This is known as bleeding or moving.

Pens with nibs are quite a challenge and tend to be better left until Year 6. White ink on black paper can look very good. Care needs to be taken when washing and drying nibs after use as they can clog up with rust.

Making different lines with fine, medium and broad line pens

Time	Resources	National Curriculum
15 min.	Fine line pens (tip size approx. 0.4 mm) Medium tip pens (approx. 0.8 mm) Broad pens, round (tip approx. 1.6 mm) and/or chisel tip (approx. 2 mm and 5 mm) Sketchbooks	2a, 4a

Warning!

If permanent pens are being used, they go through the paper onto the next page in the sketchbook, or onto the table if you are working on paper. Put some newspaper underneath.

Introduction

'You are going to investigate and record all the different lines that can be made with these pens. They have different thicknesses and will make different kinds of lines. You will do this in your sketchbooks as a useful reference. You will be able to look back to see which pens would be best for which drawing activities.'

Practical activity

❑ Put out a selection of pens of different sizes on their tables.

❑ Using the same types of lines as in the pencil skill lesson (page 20), ask the children to try out all these kinds of lines with each size of pen.

❑ Explain that the pens with the chisel tip can make a broad or narrow line according to how the pen is angled on the paper.

❑ Encourage children to mix the pen lines, crossing fine lines over broad lines.

❑ You could ask them to suggest suitable subjects for each type of pen. For example, *'I think if I were drawing a feather, I would use a fine line pen.'*

Year 5 child's experimentations with different types of line

 USING SKILL

Fine, medium and broad line pens

Time	Resources	National Curriculum
30 min. approx.	Fine, medium and broad pens Sketchbooks or large paper if work is to be done in a group	1a, 2a, 4a

Introduction

'Now that you have experimented making different types of line using different pens, you are going to do a drawing using all three pen sizes. You can decide the subject, and which things would be best drawn with which pen.'

Practical activity

❐ The classroom is a good subject as there are items of various scales all in the one context.

❐ Children could work collaboratively in a group, drawing different aspects of the room from different angles.

❐ Draw attention to small detail such as sockets, locks and door handles and larger-scale items like the framework of the room itself or larger furniture.

❐ Remind children to use the different pens for different aspects of the room.

❐ Colour could be added later to enhance the drawing.

USING SKILL

Fine line pens

Time	Resources	National
30 min.	Fine line pens (0.4 mm and/or 0.3 mm tip)	Curriculum
	Sketchbooks	1a, 2a, 4a
	Small-scale artefacts with intricate detail such as:	
	leaves, flowers, feathers, shells, lace; topic artefacts	
	Magnifying glasses	
	To add colour: water or watercolours and fine	
	watercolour brushes	

Introduction
'You will be using fine line pens today, which are excellent for drawing small, delicate or detailed subjects.'

Practical activity
❑ Children should look carefully at the shapes, patterns and textures before starting to draw. They could use magnifying glasses.
❑ They should think about how they will place the drawing on the paper before they start, then put in as much detail as they can.
❑ Draw children's attention to the shapes and variety of lines on the subjects.
❑ Explain that they should not do any solid filling in as this is a line drawing and they will do that later.

Adding water and/or colour to drawings
❑ Most fine line pens are water-based. Lovely effects can be achieved by wetting the lines with the tip of a small watercolour brush. The black ink will 'move' and areas of tone are created. The black becomes a soft dark brown. Other colours can be added to this.
❑ The drawings could be photocopied and then painted using watercolours.

Example of a drawing that was photocopied and painted using watercolours

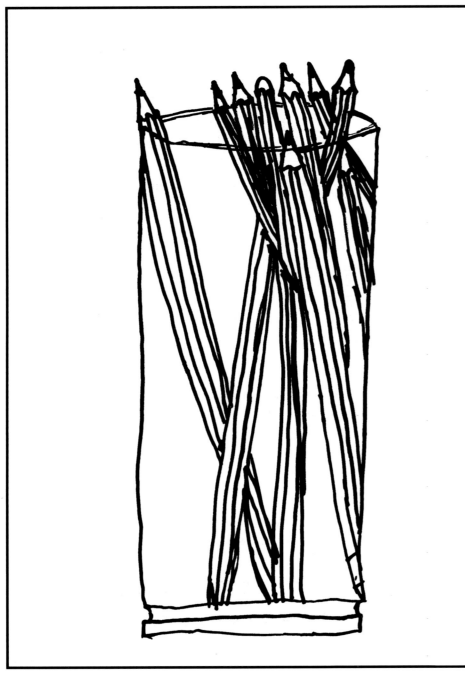

Bethan Vanstone, Year 5

 USING SKILL

Medium line pens

Time	Resources	National Curriculum
20 min.	Medium pens (up to approx. 0.8 mm tip) Sketchbooks Collection of suitable artefacts with minimal detail (topic-related or from around the classroom: pots of pens, brushes, stacks of books)	1a, 2a, 4a

Introduction
'Medium tip pens make a good strong line. They are very useful when you are drawing quickly. They will allow you to do some detail, but not as much as a fine line pen.'

Practical activity
❏ Ask the children to suggest objects they think would look good drawn with a medium pen.
❏ Guide their choices.
❏ Tell the children to:
   ✻ Think carefully about where you will begin your drawing. Once you have started there is no going back, and you cannot alter your drawings easily
   ✻ Think about the way you will place the drawing on the paper, the main shapes you can see, and how the finished drawing might look
❏ Look for the lines around the outside and within the artefact. When drawings are finished, ask children to consider if they have used the pens well or if they could have achieved better results with a different size of pen.

USING SKILL

Broad line pens

Time	Resources	National
20 min.	Broad pens (size 1.6 mm upward) round tip and/or chisel tips Sketchbooks	**Curriculum** 1a, 2a, 4a

Warning!
Permanent pens go through the page so you might prefer to work on paper with newspaper underneath.

Introduction
'Broad pens are brilliant when you want to do large, dramatic or bold drawings. You won't be able to draw much detail, but you will be able to make simple clear bold lines that can make your drawings look strong and dramatic.'

Practical activity
❐ Guide the children's choices of subject matter: classroom furniture, the school hall, the outside of the school, large leafless trees and telegraph poles are all good subjects.

❐ Tell the children that they must think carefully before they start to draw and to consider how the drawing will fit on the page. They will need to get the scale right.

❐ Once they have started to draw encourage them to keep up a good pace and to be bold.

❐ When they have completed their drawings ask them if they think they could have drawn the same subject as well, and created the same effect, with a fine line pen.

Background information
Broad pens are excellent for group work and for bold large-scale drawings. The advantage of permanent pens is that paint can be added without the pen lines running. The round tip pens are more manageable for younger pupils than the chisel tips. Year 6 could be encouraged to make both broad and medium lines using the different sides of a chisel tip pen.

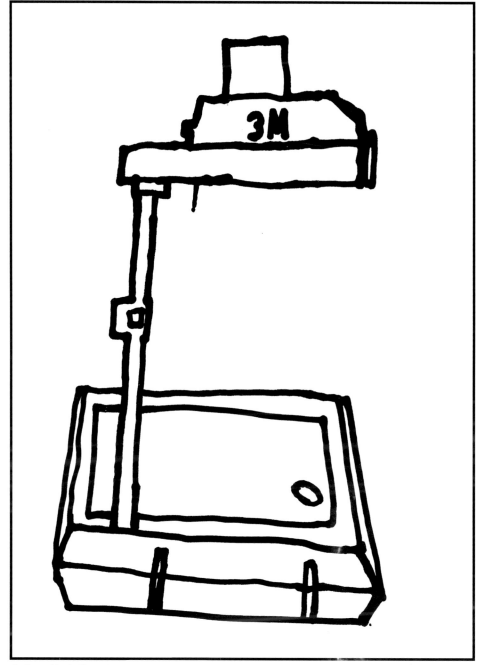

Callum Clark, Year 5

Year 6 children's examples of different types of line

| **SKILL** | Drawing lines with different character |

Drawing lines with different character

Time	Resources	National
20 min.	Sketchbooks	**Curriculum**
	Any B pencil	1c, 2a, 4a, 4b,
	List of line types (see following page)	4c

Introduction
'Lines not only have different shapes and tones, but also different characters. Artists use this knowledge to help them create a specific mood or effect.'

Practical activity
❏ Suggest two or three examples of moods or characters, e.g. angry, delicate, feeble, bold.
❏ Brainstorm more and ask the children how they think they could portray these moods or characters in line.
❏ Children now make a collection of lines in their sketchbooks, and label them.
❏ Remind them that they can use the side or the point of the pencil, light, dark, thick, thin or broken lines.

Background information
The aim of this activity is to develop children's awareness that lines can have different characters and moods. It is really a 'sowing seeds' activity, rather than one that you would expect to bear fruit immediately. It can go well with looking at line in works of art (see pages 23–25). It will help the children understand that artists have many ways to communicate.

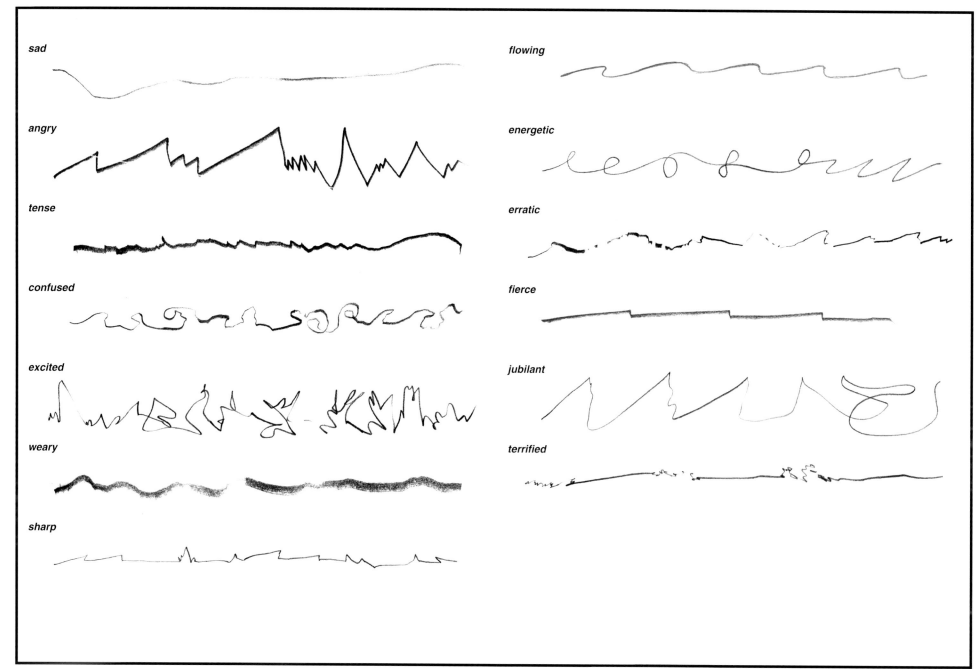

Suggestions for mood or character lines (done by author)

Using line to create tone
Single-hatching and cross-hatching

Time	Resources	National
30 min.	Sketchbooks	**Curriculum**
	Fine line pens	2b, 4a
	B, 2B and 4B pencils	
	Resource sheet 7 (page 159)	

Introduction
'There are different ways of creating tone in drawing. When this is done with lines it is called shading. Shading will help your drawings to look as if they have some solidness and depth. Shading drawn with single lines is called single-hatching and shading made with crossed lines is called cross-hatching.'

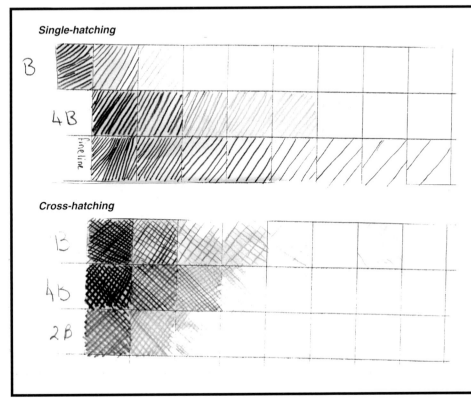

Practical activity
❏ Show the examples of single- and cross-hatching on Resource sheet 7 (page 159).
❏ Children create some kind of framework for recording the hatching: a series of boxes is fine, or children might like to devise their own.

Single-hatching
❏ With fine line pen first, draw diagonal lines close together.
❏ Repeat in the next box but draw lines a little further apart.
❏ Continue to increase the spaces between the lines.

Cross-hatching
❏ Repeat the activity as for single-hatching, but have two sets of lines crossing diagonally in each box.
❏ Now do the same with the pencils, but you can also introduce the idea that the lines can become slightly lighter in each box, as well as further apart.
❏ Children draw some simple building shapes, e.g. roof and walls. Suggest they use different degrees of hatching for each side.
❏ They should then be able to see how hatching can create the illusion of three dimensions.

Potential pitfall!
Children tend to draw hatching lines too far apart so it looks like netting.

Background information
Single-hatching is made up of a series of single lines, usually drawn at an angle; cross-hatching consists of a series of lines which cross each other – these are used to create tone or shading. It will help children to see the different depths and types of tone possible in single- and cross-hatching if they see some examples of this in the work of other artists. There are more examples of single- and cross-hatching on Resource sheets 4 and 5 (pages 156–157).

USING SKILL

Single- and cross-hatching

Time	Resources	National
30 min.	Sketchbooks	**Curriculum**
	Fine line pens or B, 2B or 4B pencils	1a, 2b, 4a
	View of some buildings (and foliage if possible)	

Introduction
'You have tried out different kinds of hatching. Now see if you can use that technique to create the illusion of solid buildings in your next drawing.'

Activity
❐ Before they draw, encourage children to see which areas have the darkest tones, medium and lightest tones as they look at their building.

❐ Remind them how they can achieve this effect with cross-hatching.

❐ Children draw the outline of the buildings.

❐ Add hatching for areas that are shadowed or darker in tone. They should include any visible foliage, trees, grass, etc. to give them scope to use different kinds of single- and cross-hatching. For example, they could use irregular lines to represent hedges or tree foliage.

Stephen Angold, Year 6

Michael McCormick, Year 6

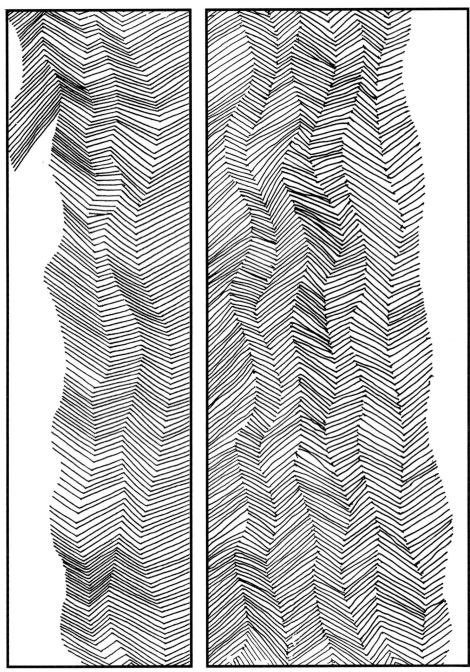

Year 6 children's examples of illusions with line

TRY THIS IDEA!

Illusions with line

Time	Resources	National
30 min. initially	HB pencils and fine line pens A4 paper or sketchbooks Enlarged copy of Resource sheet 8 (page 160)	**Curriculum** 4a, 5d

Introduction
'Lines can be drawn in such a way as to give the illusion of movement. They can deceive your eyes. Today you are going to create this effect.'

Activity 1
❏ First model covering the paper with horizontal light wavy lines in pencil.
❏ Explain that the lines should follow the waves of the line above, like the grain in wood or moving water.
❏ Children draw the wavy lines.

❏ Model the next part of the activity on the board.
❏ Using pens, children draw diagonal lines connecting the first two pencil lines. The pen lines must not touch.

- Repeat this with the row below, but with the pen lines angled the other way so they meet the lines from the row above in a 'V'.
- Continue down the page.

Activity 2

- Draw concentric circles in decreasing circumference.
- Draw diagonal lines in alternating directions in each ring.
- Create a border and infill this with diagonal lines.
- Fill background with lines radiating from the centre.
- Draw diagonals at alternating angles.
- This activity can be completed in one go, or can be added to over a period of time.

Potential pitfall!

If the pen lines touch the illusion of movement is lost.

Background information

This activity is just to give children a taste of how lines can give the illusion of movement and depth. Resource sheet 8 gives an excellent example of this. Another artist to look at is Bridget Riley.

Jack Perham, Year 6

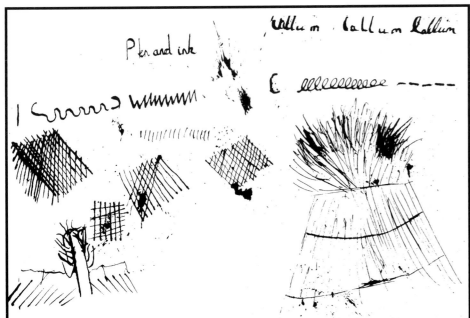

Top: Sarah Vanstone, Year 6; bottom: Callum Clark, Year 6

SKILL

Pens with nibs 1

Time	Resources	National Curriculum
15 min.	Sketchbooks or good-quality paper Pens with nibs Ink or strong dilution of dark colour Brusho (see Glossary) Copies of pen and ink drawings and/or Resource sheets 3 and 4 (pages 155–156) Tissues (for soaking up blots) Correction fluid (for covering blots!)	2a, 2b, 4a, 5d

Introduction

'Pen and ink is a classic drawing medium which has been used for centuries by countless artists. Today you are going to draw in ink using pens with nibs.'

Practical activity

❐ Show children copies of drawings done in pen and ink (Resource sheets 3 and 4).

❐ Discuss the different qualities of lines in ink compared to those of pencil, charcoal or felt tip lines.

❐ Warn children about ink blots and how to avoid them (see Background information).

❐ Children try out a range of different lines on their own. When they have achieved a few, and managed to control the worst of the blots, suggest they try single- or cross-hatching (see page 34).

❐ They can try handwriting patterns, or their own name in joined-up writing.

Background information

Drawing using pens with nibs is quite challenging and could be considered more appropriate for Year 6. Children can become quite frustrated, as the nibs tend to divide and produce a double line. Warn them to draw lightly to avoid this. Also, ink blots may splatter the page. Suggest they stroke the nib on the side of the ink container to remove the excess ink. Dab any blots with the edge of a tissue. If it has happened on a masterpiece, the blot could be covered with correction fluid once the ink has dried. After the activity the nibs need to be washed and dried as they may rust.

Pens with nibs 2

USING SKILL

Time	Resources	National Curriculum
30–45 min.	Pens with nibs Ink or strong Brusho (see Glossary) Collection of artefacts: teasels, seed heads, twiggy plants, etc. (see list on page 77) Tissues (for soaking up blots) Correction fluid (for covering blots!) Could try white ink on stiff black paper	1a, 2a, 2b, 4a 5d

Introduction

'Pen and ink are an excellent medium for drawing from nature.'

Practical activity

❐ Ask children what kind of subject matter they think would suit the medium.

❐ Let them try some of their ideas. They could annotate their drawing with comments.

❐ Then give out a collection of small artefacts. The natural world is an easy one. Try dandelion heads, spiders or dead leaves.

Background information

When children have gained some control over this medium, some of them might like to try white ink on black paper; it can look very effective. The white ink is, for some reason, harder to control than black, and the pen nibs need to be thoroughly washed and dried afterwards.

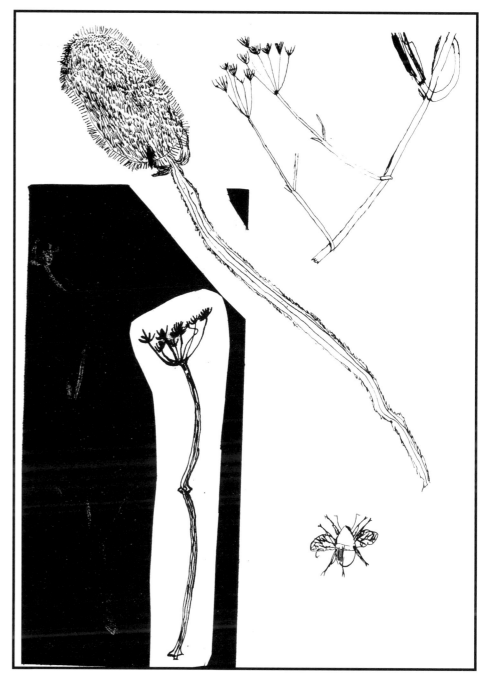

Teasels: Jade Tanton, Year 6; bee: Sarah Vanstone, Year 6

Year 6 child's example

SKILL

Making different lines with charcoal

Time	Resources	National
10 min.	Willow charcoal, two thicknesses if possible, broken into different lengths	**Curriculum**
	A3 paper or sketchbooks	2a, 4a
	Fixative (see Glossary)	
	Scrap paper to cover drawings as they progress	
	Cotton buds	
	Large piece of white paper for teacher modelling	

Introduction
'Today you will be investigating and recording all the different kinds of lines you can make using charcoal. Charcoal is the oldest known drawing medium. It is made from specially burnt wood and will break easily. It makes wonderful dark lines, but can make light ones too. One of its special qualities is that it smudges, allowing you to create misty, smoky effects.'

Practical activity
❐ Model the different kinds of line that can be made using the point and the side of the charcoal.

❐ Explain that, if the pieces of charcoal are different lengths, lines using the side of the sticks will vary too.

❐ Challenge children to make very light lines, delicate lines, lines that vary in character as they move across the paper.

❐ Remind them that dots are tiny lines, and to do some light and dark dots.

❐ Children could:
* Do some dots at speed so they become dashes
* Try single- and cross-hatching (see page 34 and Glossary)
* Smudge some lines using a cotton bud.

❐ Fix the drawings with fixative when the children are out of the room.

Background information
Further information on charcoal can be found in the Chalk and charcoal chapter, pages 134–136.

USING SKILL

Drawing with charcoal

Time	Resources	National
30 min.	Charcoal, two sizes if possible	**Curriculum**
	Sketchbooks	1a, 2a, 4a
	Resource sheets 9 and 10 (pages 161–162)	
	Fixative (see Glossary)	
	Scrap paper for covering work as it progresses	

Introduction

'Charcoal is an excellent medium for sketching; it lends itself to dramatic subjects, such as windswept landscapes, or large buildings.'

Practical activity

❑ Show children examples of charcoal drawings (see Resource sheets 9 and 10).

❑ If they are able to go outside to draw, ask what lines children think would be good for what effect. For example, what kind of line would be good for rain, grass blowing or wind swirling?

❑ Remind them to use both the side and the point of the charcoal and to make lines of different darkness and character.

❑ Suggest lightly sketching the scene before building up detail and shading.

❑ If it is not possible to go outside, then set up a large-scale still life; drape a boldly patterned fabric over tables and/or chairs, or make a collection of school plants.

❑ Draw attention to the lines and shapes that can be seen.

❑ Children lightly sketch the whole composition before adding detail and shading.

❑ Fix the charcoal drawings with fixative when the children are out of the room.

❑ Charcoal photocopies very well. Colour can then be added.

Danny Hudson, Year 6 (charcoal drawing of foliage, photocopied, then painted)

Year 5 child's example

 SKILL

Scraper technique 1

Time	Resources	National
1 hour	Cartridge paper (see Glossary)	**Curriculum**
	Coloured crayons	2a, 4a
	Oil pastels (optional)	
	Cocktail sticks or paper clips	

Introduction
'If you cover a piece of paper with two thick layers of different coloured crayon you can scrape out a picture using a small stick or thumbnail. The first colour is revealed when you scrape off the second one. It takes quite a lot of time to prepare the background but the effects can be really good.'

Practical activity
❑ Show the children the examples of children's work from this book and explain the technique.

❑ First cover the paper with a good layer of crayon. This can be single or multicoloured, depending on what effect you want to achieve.

❑ Next cover this with a thick solid layer of dark crayon or oil pastel. (Oil pastels are softer and the layer is slightly easier to apply than with crayon.)

❑ If the top layer is crayon, it can be polished to make a really smooth solid surface.

❑ Lines and patterns can be scraped off using a cocktail stick. Paper clips with one end unwound make good scrapers.

❑ It might help children to get the feel of how it works if they do a small test piece first.

❑ They could try out dark base layers with light top layers and vice versa.

❑ These investigations could then be stuck in their sketchbooks and annotated.

Year 6 child's experimentation with different coloured backgrounds and different techniques (see colour version on front cover)

Background information
Scraper work is really first cousin to printing, having links with etching. However, as primary children are most unlikely to have experience of etching, it fits quite well here in the Line chapter. It enables the children to see line in a different colour context. It gives line a new dimension.

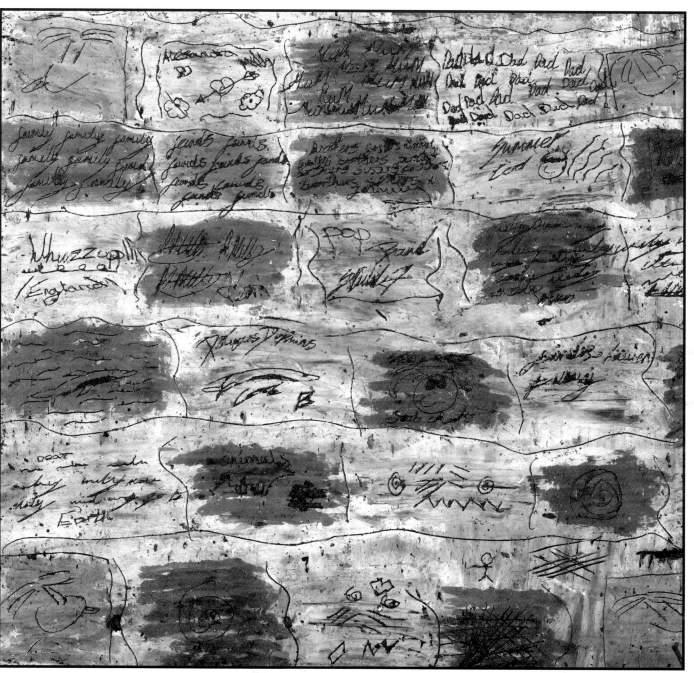

Alexandra Mills, Year 6 (test page of different combinations of colours)

Jordan Clark, Year 5

Hope Alexander, Year 5

 USING SKILL

Scraper technique 2

Time	Resources	National
1 hour	Cartridge paper (see Glossary)	**Curriculum**
	Coloured crayons	1a, 2a, 4a
	Oil pastels (optional)	
	Cocktail sticks	
	Enlarged copy of Paul Klee's drawings and/or	
	Resource sheet 11 (page 163)	

Introduction

'You have investigated different effects with the scraper technique. Now you are going to create a picture using it.'

Practical activity

❐ Before children embark on their pictures, ask them to consider whether they might like to use more than one colour for the lower layer of crayon. It will depend on the subject matter. They need to have roughly planned their designs before applying the bottom layer of colour.

❐ Paul Klee's picture, 'They're biting' (Resource sheet 11) is a good stimulus; although it wasn't created using the scraper technique it looks as if it was. Another good stimulus is Paul Klee's 'Growth in an Old Garden'.

❐ If there is no natural link to another subject area, the themes of night-time, underwater, fireworks, outer space or fantasy creatures can look great.

❐ Ideas could be tried out in sketchbooks.

Background information

A5 is probably the largest size to work with, as children can get discouraged covering larger areas with crayon.

Tone

Year 5 children's pencil tone drawings

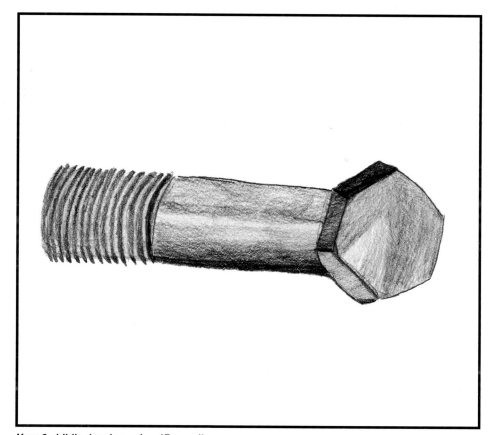

Year 6 child's drawing using 4B pencil

Tone

Rationale

The lightness or darkness of a colour, such as the shades of grey in the gradual change from black to white, is called tone.

Children can use tone to create the illusion of form and solidity, to create mood or to direct the viewer's attention.

Tone can make the whole effect of a drawing more dramatic, atmospheric and interesting.

The gradual transition of tone from light to dark was once regarded as essential to good drawing.

What is tone?

Artists sometimes use the term 'value' to describe the lightness or darkness of a colour. Children can find it hard to understand that colours have a tone. With black it is easier to accept: there is black, there is white and there is the whole range between.

It can help children to understand that colours also have a tonal value if they are asked to visualize black and white films, when colour is translated into various tones of black to white. Or they could be shown a coloured picture and then a photocopy of the same picture.

Tone can be linear, that is, created by line as in single- or cross-hatching (see page 34 and Glossary.)

When tone is created by a series of close lines, it is sometimes known as shading, although shading can be created in a number of ways. Some of the most subtle tonal effects are made by blending or smudging.

Tone can make the whole effect of a drawing more interesting and dramatic. Children can use tone to create the illusion of form and space.

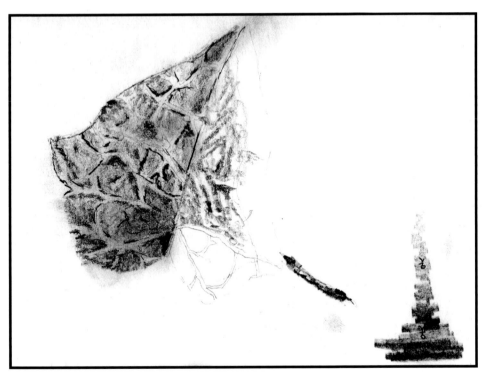

Year 6 child's tonal drawing

'Light and shadows should blend without line or borders, in the manner of smoke.'
Leonardo da Vinci
Treatise on Painting

46

About this chapter

In this chapter children will learn how to make different tones in soft pencil and charcoal.

They will try to create the illusion of form and weight using different tones in pencil and charcoal.

They will learn to perceive the different tones in the world around them.

They will use these tones in different contexts to create the illusion of form, weight or movement.

If you only have time for one skill, do the key skill.

Year 5 child's tonal drawing of Edgard Degas's Cafe-concert at the Ambassadeurs, 1876-77

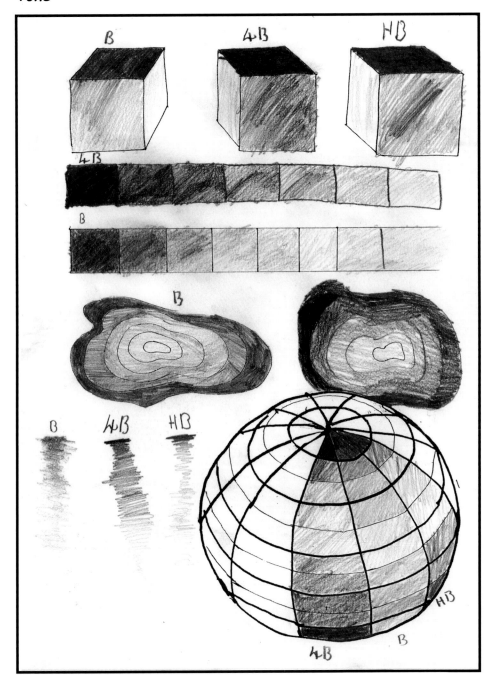

Year 6 child's completed Resource sheet 12

 KEY SKILL

Making different tones in pencil

Time	Resources	National
30–40 min.	Sketchbooks	Curriculum
	Resource sheet 12 (page 164), one per child	1c, 2b, 4a
	Selection of art pencils, varying grades between 2H and 6B	
	Coloured pencils (art quality if possible)	
	Large sheet of paper to model tones	
	Example of a line drawing and a tone drawing	

Introduction

Revise definition of tone (see page 46), then say to the children, *'Tone can help your drawings look more three-dimensional.'* (Here you could show the line and tone drawing examples and make comparisons.) *'Tone can also help give your drawings a mood or atmosphere, for example, a gloomy castle or a misty morning. Today you are going to try out all the different tones you can make with different grades of pencil.'*

Practical activity

❏ Demonstrate some of the tones that can be made with one of the B pencils, showing how tone can gradually change from dark to light.

❏ Explain that to make the darkest tones you press more heavily with the pencil; to make lighter tones you use much less pressure.

❏ Children then try this with the different grades of pencil.

❏ They decide how they are going to record these in a systematic way, labelling the grades of pencil. They could use Resource sheet 12, as illustrated on this page.

❏ They investigate tone with coloured pencils in the same way. This helps to reinforce the idea that colour has a tonal scale.

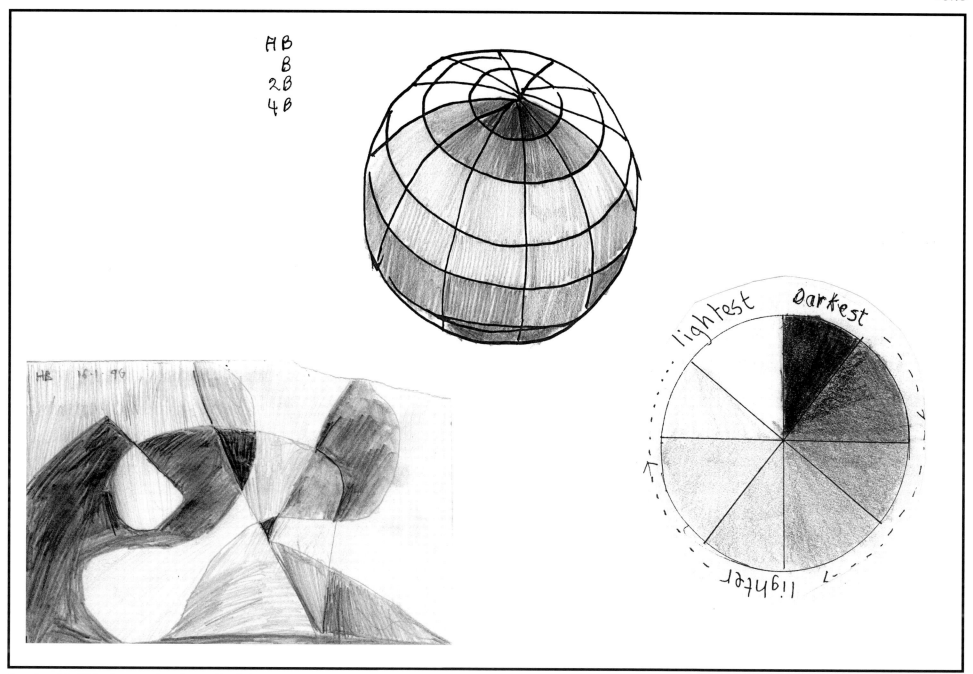

HB
B
2B
4B

Year 5 and 6 children's examples of recording in tone

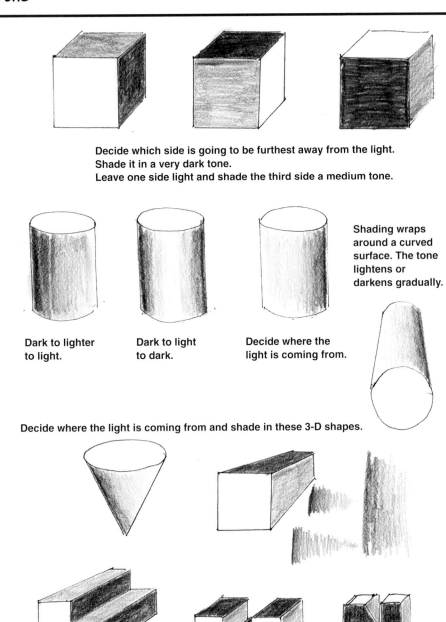

Decide which side is going to be furthest away from the light.
Shade it in a very dark tone.
Leave one side light and shade the third side a medium tone.

Shading wraps around a curved surface. The tone lightens or darkens gradually.

Dark to lighter to light.

Dark to light to dark.

Decide where the light is coming from.

Decide where the light is coming from and shade in these 3-D shapes.

Year 6 child's completed Resource sheet 13

Using tone to shade three-dimensional shapes

Time	Resources	National
30 min.	Sketchbooks	Curriculum
	B, 2B or 4B pencils	1a, 4a
	Selection of three-dimensional shapes: cones, spheres, cubes (maths shapes are preferable, as they have no distracting patterns)	
	Resource sheet 13 (page 165) for children who find drawing three-dimensional shapes too challenging	

Introduction
'You have investigated making different tones with a variety of pencils.
Now you are going to use tone to make flat shapes look three-dimensional.'

Practical activity
Teacher
❒ Hold up each of the three-dimensional shapes in turn and point out where the light falls, and how it changes when the shape is rotated.

❒ Draw attention to the tone changing gradually around the curved surfaces of the sphere, cone and cylinder.

❒ Point out shadows caused by the shapes and ask children to include these in their drawings to help create the illusion of depth and space.

Children
❒ Resource sheet 13 can be used by children who find drawing three-dimensional shapes too challenging.

❒ If they are drawing their own shapes, they need to draw three of each.

❒ Shade each cube with the light coming from different directions.

❒ Suggest each cube has one light, one medium and one dark surface.

- Before shading the cylinders children should be told:
  * To decide each time where the light is coming from
  * Tone should change from dark to light gradually as the shadow creeps across the shape – that this is a key factor in creating convincing shading
  * Shading should be drawn along the length of the cylinder
  * To decide whether the top or base of the cylinder is in shadow.
- Similar rules apply when shading the cone.
- Having done this they might like to make some letters look three-dimensional.

Potential pitfalls!

If children don't shade gradually from dark to light, the cylinder will look striped rather than three-dimensional. If shading is drawn across, rather than along the length of the cylinder, it will tend to flatten it.

Background information
The fading out of line can be achieved in a number of ways. Smudging or blending with a finger is probably the most manageable. Blending can also be done with a tissue or piece of cotton wool. Tone for darker areas can be built up in layers. Lighter areas can be created by lifting off with an eraser. This is very useful when putting highlights on a sphere. Erasers can be useful also for softening the edges. However, there is always the problem that once children have an eraser they tend to rub out more than they draw.

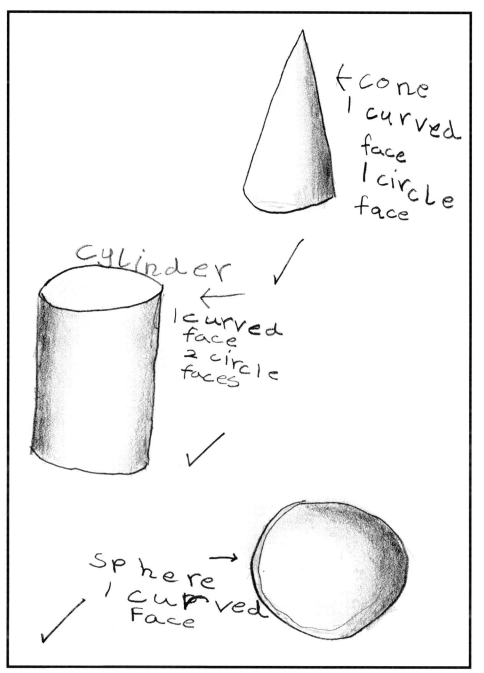

Jessica Pearson, Year 5

51

Daisy Perham, Year 5 (making tones from a newspaper picture)

 USING SKILL

Making different tones in pencil 1

Time	Resources	National Curriculum
15 min.	Sketchbooks 2B or 4B pencils Pictures from newspapers showing speed and movement such as footballers, horses galloping, fast cars or motorbikes cut out and stuck into sketchbooks (children can do this themselves)	1a, 2a, 4a, 5a

Introduction
'You have investigated making different tones with pencils and have shaded some shapes to make them look three-dimensional. Now you are going to use those skills. In this activity, you are going to try to match some tones to give the impression of movement and speed.'

Practical activity
❏ Children stick a newspaper picture in their sketchbooks, leaving a space behind the picture for the tone slipstream.

❏ Ask them to decide which is the darkest tone, next darkest, lightest tone, next lightest.

❏ Children then try to match the tone with their pencils. Suggest they shade in the tone horizontally so it looks as if the subject in the picture is moving and the shading is a kind of slipstream behind it. You could show them the example in this book.

❏ Remind children that their real job is to look carefully and match the tones as closely as they can.

USING SKILL

Making different tones in pencil 2

Time	Resources	National
30–40 min.	Sketchbooks	**Curriculum**
	2B or 4B pencils	2a, 2b, 4a
	Collection of heavy metal objects: nuts, bolts, screws, tools (see page 77 for list)	

Introduction
'Now you are going to draw some of these objects' (show them some of the metal objects) *'...and try to make them look really solid and heavy.'*

Practical activity
❏ Give children a chunky metal object to draw, preferably one each.
❏ Children draw the outline quite lightly, scaling it up if necessary.
❏ Ask children to consider where the light comes from and how the shadows fall.
❏ Ask them to look at the darkest area and shade that in first.
❏ Now children need to note the lightest areas and leave these light. They then add any other tones they can see.
❏ Explain that they can blend the tones by smudging, and that they can also add lines over tones towards the end of the drawing to give the object definition.
❏ Lastly draw any shadow cast by the object, which will help give it the illusion of solidness.

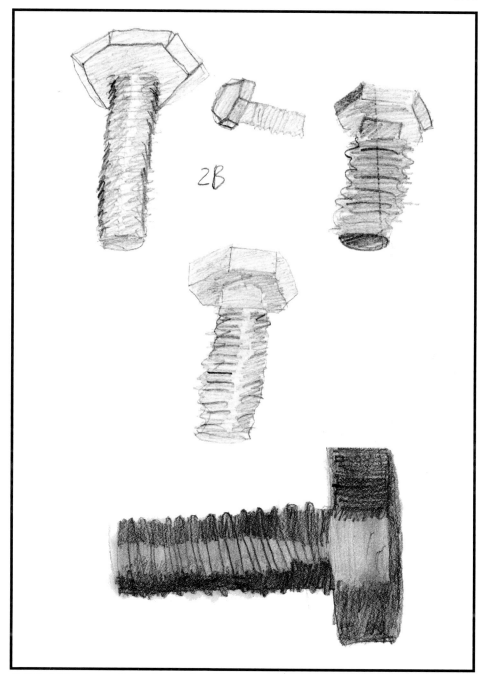

Year 6 children's pencil drawings, using different tones

Year 5 child's recording of charcoal tones

 SKILL # Making different tones with charcoal

Time	Resources	National Curriculum
15–20 min.	Charcoal, two different thicknesses if possible, broken into 4 cm pieces Some old erasers Fixative (see Glossary) Scrap paper Copies of Resource sheet 14 (page 166)	2a, 2b, 4a

Introduction

'Charcoal is made of specially burned wood. It has been a drawing medium since the days of the cave people. It makes dramatic dark marks, it smudges and it is ideal for quick bold drawings. Today you are going to make different tones in charcoal. You can create highlights by removing areas of tone with an eraser.'

Practical activity

❏ Children experiment with charcoal to produce as many different tones as possible, first with the point of the charcoal and then the side.

❏ Tell them to blend some marks by smudging, and see if they can phase out the tone so it becomes almost invisible.

❏ They can create different tones by drawing lines close together and then smudging them, or by light feather strokes which are then blended. Year 5 should make at least eight different tones, some may make a lot more. Year 6 should make twelve.

❏ Children could create their tones on Resource sheet 14, or they could invent their own grid.

❏ Children could draw a circle in charcoal and then shade it in gradually, lightening the tone as they get nearer the middle so that it now looks like a sphere.

❏ They can experiment with lifting areas of tone with erasers, and adding dark backgrounds behind shaded cubes and spheres.

Background information

To make sure work is not spoiled by being smudged as work progresses, provide the children with a piece of scrap paper that can be laid over any completed sections of their work. Snap the charcoal into short lengths, about 4 cm – this will enable them to draw with the side as well as the point. Drawings can be sprayed with fixative when the children have left the room.

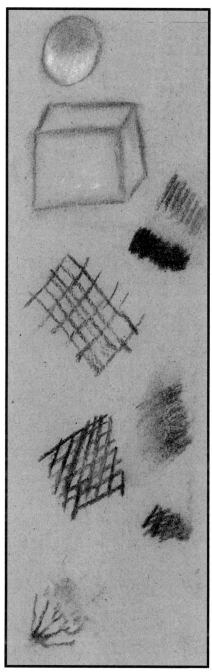

Year 5 child's tones

Year 5 child's tones

55

USING SKILL Creating tone with charcoal

Time	Resources	National Curriculum
30–45 min.	Charcoal, broken into 4 cm pieces Sketchbooks or slightly off-white paper Old erasers View/scene to sketch Scrap paper if working indoors Fixative (see Glossary) Digital camera (optional)	1a, 1c, 2a, 4a, 5a

Introduction
'You have been investigating different tones you can make with charcoal. Now you are going to have the opportunity to use those effects in your drawings.'

Practical activity
❏ Children make a quick light outline of their subject, with no detail.

❏ Ask where the darkest and lightest areas are. They could try half closing their eyes to get an overall image. Sometimes it is easier to see the main tonal contrasts this way.

❏ Suggest they block the darkest areas in first.

❏ Then build up the rest of the picture, filling in with different tones, leaving out the lightest areas. The paper acts as the lightest tone.

❏ Remind them they can use an eraser to remove tone.

❏ Line detail and textures could then be added last.

Extension idea
❏ If you have a digital camera, you could photograph the subject, print it out, photocopy it so it becomes black and white, and enlarge it.

❏ Then children can compare their tonal picture against the photocopy. Their pictures and the photocopies could be mounted and displayed side by side.

Victoria Braund, Year 5

Texture

Ahmed Razak, Year 6

Poppy Bell, Year 6

Texture

Rationale

Texture is the word that explains how things feel when we touch them. In drawing it is the marks on a surface which represent the way textures look.

Textural surfaces are appreciated through both touch and sight.

Texture can add interest and definition to a drawing. Children can use drawn texture to create the illusion of difference between one surface and another, for example fur and skin, wood and stone.

They can use texture to give their drawings variety and interest and to differentiate between one area and another, and to create contrast.

About this chapter

In this chapter children will record ways of representing textures, using different drawing media on different papers. They will then use some of these techniques, drawing from first-hand observations.

Year 5 child's drawing of knitted soft toy frog

Rebecca Lumb, Year 5

58

Drawing different textures

Time	Resources	National Curriculum
30 min.	Sketchbooks Variety of drawing media: B or 2B pencils, felt tips, crayons, ball-point pens Range of different papers, cut into squares (different weights of cartridge, tracing, brown wrapping paper) Collection of artefacts that have different textures: shells, orange peel, bark, fur, sacking, rough stone Large piece of white paper for teacher modelling	1a, 1c, 2a, 2b 4a, 4b

Introduction

'You are going to be looking at, feeling and drawing different textures today. Texture is a word that explains how things feel when we touch them. You can both see and feel textures. Even the surfaces you draw on have a texture.'

Practical activity

❑ First model ways to record some textures, e.g. dots for sandpaper, little dashes for fur, scribbly lines for wool.

❑ Give out textured objects and allow a few minutes for children to feel the items and talk about them.

❑ Children then make a series of marks to represent the texture of each artefact.

❑ Suggest they make the marks in different media and on different papers, and write words describing the textures.

❑ The different paper samples can be stuck into their sketchbooks and annotated.

Background information

Texture refers to surface quality. All materials have their own textural quality. Texture is appreciated through both touch and sight. Here the children will be concerned with creating the illusion of texture by making marks. Rubbings are a way of recording textures. In this lesson children work out which drawn marks give the impression of texture and become aware that drawing surfaces have different textures. It will be easier for children to draw textures if they collect a range of marks that can represent textured surfaces.

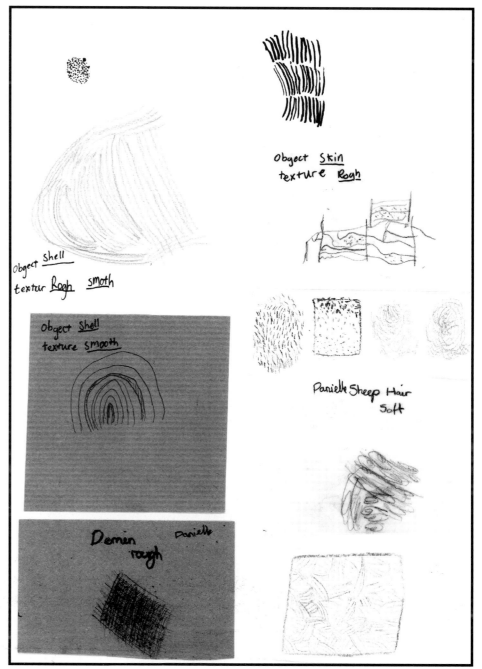

Year 5 child's example of textures on different types of papers

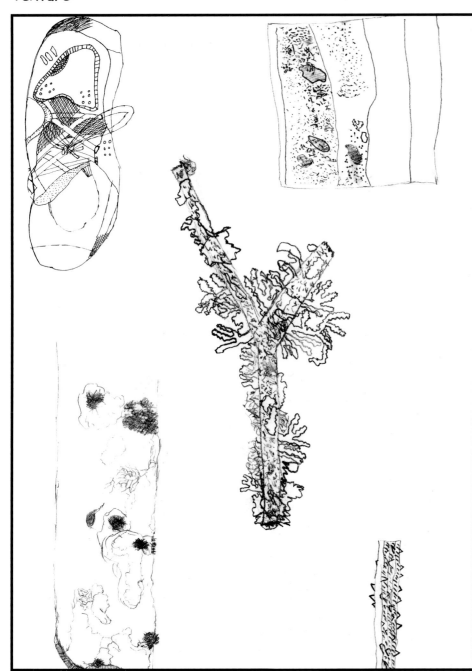

Middle plant: Sam Jeffrey, Year 5; other artists not known

USING SKILL — Drawing textures

Time	Resources	National Curriculum
30 min.	Sketchbooks Variety of drawing media: B or 2B pencils, ball-point pens, felt tips, crayons, charcoal (all black if possible) Artefacts with textured surfaces: shells, twigs with bark, shoes, mossy stones (see list on page 77) Children could draw themselves or each other Papers with different surface textures (optional)	1a, 1c, 2a, 2b, 2c, 4a

Introduction
'Using texture in your drawings helps to make them more interesting visually. You can use line, tone, and texture to help create the effect you want. Contrasting textures look especially good.'

Practical activity
❐ Put a selection of different drawing media on the tables.
❐ Discuss the textures on items to be drawn, and the media that would be most suitable for the subject matter.
❐ If children are drawing themselves or each other, draw attention to all the different textures: skin, different clothing materials, hair. Very short hair has a different texture from long or curly hair; leather shoes have a different texture from fabric trainers.
❐ Children might want to use more than one drawing medium within the same drawing to achieve a particular effect. They might try the same drawing, but on different papers.
❐ Children lightly draw the outline of the subject, then draw in as many different textures as they can see, using whatever marks they think appropriate.
❐ Draw their attention to the fact that one subject or artefact may have several textures.
❐ Ask children to look for interesting contrasts of textures, like a stone with moss or where the fabric of a sleeve meets the skin of their hands. They could do a sketch of just that part.
❐ Suggest they try shading with the side of the pencil to create a tonal background and then add texture over this.

Pattern

Year 5 child's repeated flower drawing – part of textile design

Year 6 child's doodle drawing

Pattern

Rationale

Investigating and making patterns is one way of developing children's aesthetic sensibilities.

Creating patterns can be a very pleasing activity. Children can build up their collections of line patterns over a period of time. They can then use them to decorate other pieces of work or they can turn the collections of patterns into works of art in their own right as in the doodle activity (pages 68–69). While they are creating their doodle children can day-dream a little. Day-dreaming is an essential element of creativity.

Once children have a range of patterns they can launch into decorative art and craft activities with greater confidence.

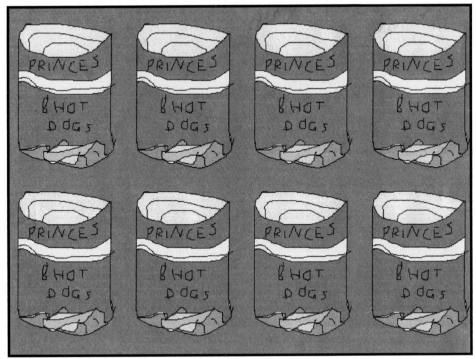

Year 5 child's computer drawn hot dogs, inspired by Andy Warhol

What is pattern?

Pattern is a repeat of lines, shapes or colours. Pattern falls roughly into three groups: regular, irregular and unintentional pattern.

Pattern in nature, regular and irregular

Pattern in nature is often irregular, like the spots on a leopard. In the case of the leopard's spots or the tiger's stripes, there is a family of shapes. We perceive them as patterns but they are in fact irregular.

Other patterns in nature are regular in shape but they vary in size, such as the whorls on a tortoise shell, the scales on a fish or the feathers on a bird. Single shapes such as the spiral on a shell can be taken and turned into a pattern. It can be the inspiration for a pattern, but on its own it is not a pattern.

Regular patterns

Regular patterns are more likely to be man-made. They are made by regular repeats of lines, shapes or colours.

The simplest pattern will consist of a single shape, line or colour, repeated in a regular way.

More complex patterns use more than one shape, line or colour. They might repeat in different ways, such as by rotating, reflecting or inverting motifs.

Unintentional pattern

Cars in a car park, books on shelves, leaves in a pile and products on supermarket shelves can create a kind of pattern because they are in families of shapes.

Pattern for decoration

Pattern is closely associated with the decorative arts – tiles, pottery, fabrics, wallpaper, tapestries, carpets – and also with folk art. From earliest times people have felt the need to decorate artefacts. Cultural traditions and fashions have defined styles, while materials and tools available have influenced the types of patterns produced.

62

Patterns are designed to fit the objects they are going to decorate; plate designs tend to be round, borders long and narrow.

Collecting, analyzing and creating patterns lead very naturally to print-making. Although in this chapter patterns will be drawn, the work will still be a very useful foundation for printing.

About this chapter

Artists are inspired by pattern in nature, so it is a good starting point for children. We are surrounded by pattern in both the natural and man-made world, so there is plenty of stimulus.

In this chapter children study how patterns are made from line and shape and how to add to these in different ways. They will make more complex patterns by rotating and reflecting motifs.

They will develop a bank of patterns that they can later apply to designs.

They will collect patterns and shapes from the natural world and use these to create a fabric or wallpaper design.

They will study the patterns used in the art and craft of different cultures.

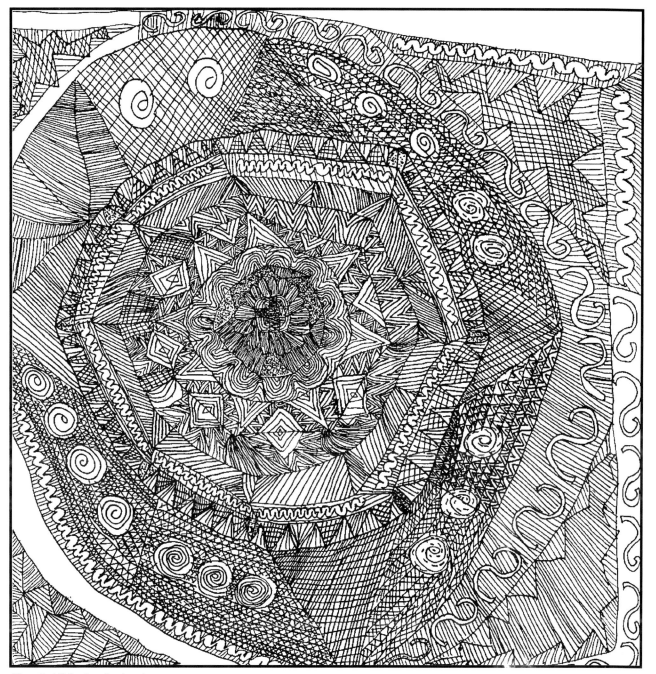

Year 6 child's doodle drawing

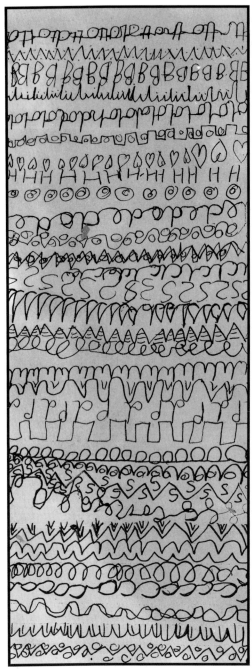

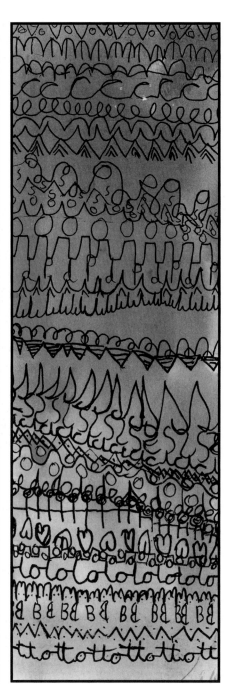

Patterns done by Year 5 children

KEY SKILL

Making patterns with lines and shapes 1

Time	Resources	National Curriculum
30 min.	Sketchbooks	1c, 3b, 4a
	Any pencil, HB will do (could use felt tips)	
	Resource sheet 15 (page 167)	
	Brusho and brushes	
	Large piece of white paper for teacher modelling	

Introduction

'Pattern is made with regular repeats of lines or shapes. Handwriting patterns are a good example of this. Today you are going to create some handwriting patterns of your own. You can use both capital and small letters, you can overlap letters, reflect or rotate them, or draw them upside down.'

Practical activity

(Model each stage first.)

☐ Linked Vs drawn continuously:

☐ Pairs of Vs:

W W W W

☐ Vs of different sizes:

☐ Overlapped Vs:

❐ Add in dots:

❐ Invert one row of Vs above another:

❐ Children try patterns using different letters.
❐ The most effective patterns could be collected onto one sheet, photocopied and stuck in their sketchbooks as a resource.
❐ The patterns can also be colour-washed and displayed.
❐ Paul Klee's picture 'Pastorale' (Resource sheet 15), which has similar patterns, is a good stimulus.

Background information
This skill is closely related to handwriting and helps improve hand–eye co-ordination. It will also develop their bank of patterns. The resulting drawings can be colour-washed with Brusho (see Glossary) and displayed.

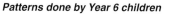

Patterns done by Year 6 children

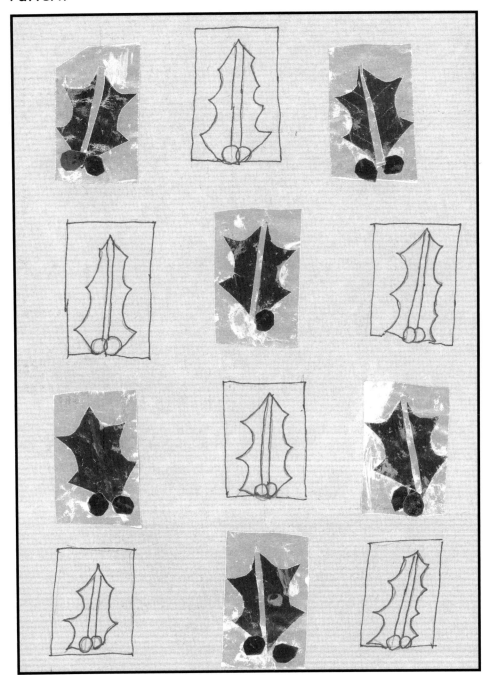

Melissa Peddar, Year 5

 KEY SKILL

Making patterns with lines and shapes 2

Time	Resources	National
30–40 min.	Sketchbooks or paper if working on larger scale	Curriculum
	Pencils or fine line pens	1c, 3b, 4a
	Coloured paper, A5 approx.	
	Glue	
	Scissors	

Introduction
'You are going to create some patterns by turning the shapes in different ways.'

Practical activity
☐ Model on the board what happens when you rotate a shape, such as a heart or leaf.

☐ Ask the children to choose a simple shape.

☐ Fold the coloured paper as many times as possible, but so it can still easily be cut through.

☐ Children draw their shape on the paper and cut it out. They will now have a number of shapes.

☐ Repeat with either the same shape in a different colour or a different shape.

☐ Children arrange the shapes on a piece of paper in five or six rows. There could be alternate shapes or colours, or alternate rows of different shapes – there are many ways they could be arranged. Don't stick them down yet.

☐ Next, tell them to turn some shapes upside down.

☐ Suggest trying different combinations: two up, two down, or all up one row and all down the next.

- ❐ They can try rotating a shape through 90 degrees. They will soon get the idea and come up with many different arrangements.
- ❐ Emphasize that the spaces between the shapes must be regular.
- ❐ When finished, they could stick their design down and draw it.
- ❐ Quite good designs for wrapping paper can be produced.

Potential pitfall!

Children find it hard to regulate the spaces between shapes. They focus on the shapes not the spaces. Discourage the sticking down of shapes until they have checked the regularity of the spacing.

Background information

It is easier for children to understand rotated and reflected repeats if they do them in cut paper first. It will also help when they use patterns in printing. There are also links with shape in maths.

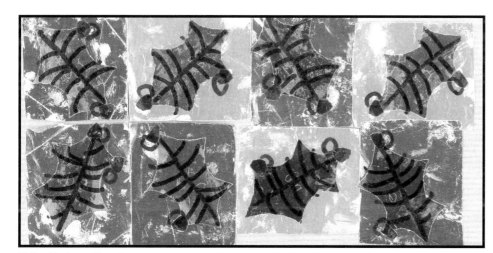

Daisy Perham, Year 5

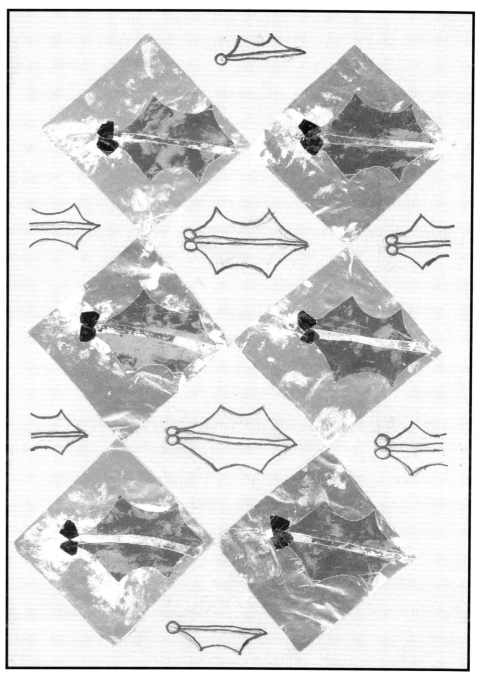

Alexandra Mills, Year 6

Using line patterns in a doodle

Time	Resources	National
15 min.	Sketchbooks or A3 paper	Curriculum
to set up	Fine felt tips or fine line pens	4a
doodle	A few enlarged examples of doodles to show	
	(pages 63 and 69)	
	Examples of doodles and handwriting patterns,	
	such as: Resource sheets 16 and 17	
	(pages 168–169)	

Practical activity

☐ Show examples of doodles on pages 63 and 69. These would look better enlarged to A3, which was their original size. This should motivate children.

☐ Explain that these doodles started with a small shape in the middle and grew very slowly, like a crystal, over some time.

☐ Emphasize that this is a line drawing activity, so no solid colouring in.

☐ Children start the doodle in the middle of the paper by drawing a simple shape, e.g. a circle, square, flower or cross.

☐ Then add to this motif, with tiny lines.

☐ Explain that every time their lines create a shape they should fill that shape in with a pattern.

☐ They could look back in their sketchbooks at the handwriting and line patterns for ideas, or at the doodle worksheet (Resource sheet 16).

☐ Remind them to work slowly and carefully. Once started, doodles can be done in odd moments, e.g. clearing-up time or during registration.

Potential pitfall!

Children will try to rush doodles at first. To give them an idea of how slowly to progress, advise them that after 10 minutes their doodle should be no bigger than a 50p piece.

Background information

Looking at pattern is an essential part of learning to draw. Creating patterns can be a very pleasing activity. As the pattern in this activity grows, so does the child's confidence and their aesthetic appreciation of pattern.

Children can build up their collections of line patterns over a period of time. They can then use them to decorate other pieces of work, or they can turn the collections of patterns into works of art in their own right, such as the doodles in this activity. Once children have a bank of patterns they can launch into decorative art and craft activities with greater confidence.

If the doodles are started on A3 paper they can last for a term, worked on for a few minutes at a time. For some reason children find them very soothing and satisfying, so they are very useful on a variety of occasions.

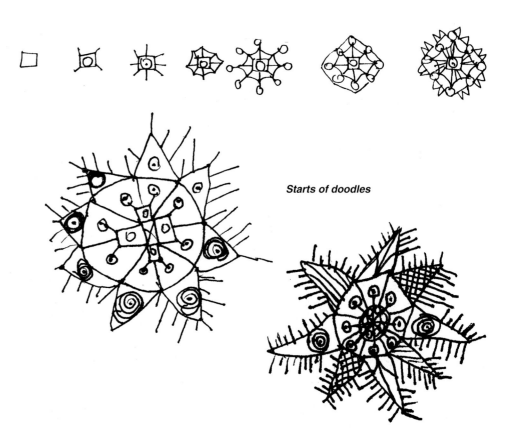

Starts of doodles

Year 5 children's drawings

Collecting patterns from nature

TRY THIS IDEA!

Time	Resources	National Curriculum
30 min.	A4 paper	
	Fine line pens (ink drawings photocopy well)	1a, 1b, 1c, 4a
	Selection of natural artefacts that have patterns: shells, leaves, fruit, vegetables, feathers, flowers	
	Magnifying glasses	

Introduction

'Patterns are repeats of lines, shapes or colours. There are natural patterns all around us. You can see patterns in waves in the sea, clouds in the sky or in the veins of a leaf. If there is a single shape or line, like the spiral on a shell, it is not a pattern. It could become one if you copied and repeated it. You are going to look at some natural patterns using the magnifying glasses. Another time you might use some of these drawings to create a fabric or wallpaper design.'

Practical activity

❐ Distribute the artefacts.

❐ Encourage children to talk about the patterns they can see.

❐ Draw a few of them on the board: the arrangement of shapes from the seed head, some lines from the leaf, and so on.

❐ Ask the children to carefully draw an artefact, including the patterns. (This drawing or a similar one might be used to create a fabric or wallpaper design in the next activity.)

❐ Next draw just the patterns. It might be useful to make a few notes about the colour for future reference, for example for a weaving or print. Encourage the children to label the patterns: e.g. 'Patterns from a beech leaf'.

❐ Children should draw as many different objects as there is time for.

Background information

Collections of patterns in sketchbooks are an invaluable resource. Children can use the patterns at some later time for decorating something, or for a project that is already in hand. For example: printing, indenting patterns on clay, or decorating a papier mâché plate.

Using patterns and shapes from nature to create designs

Time	Resources	National Curriculum
45 min.	Sketchbooks Scissors Glue Fabrics or wallpaper designs based on natural forms and/or Copy of Resource sheet 18 (page 170) for each child Several photocopies of a drawing by each child from previous lesson (might be reduced) Several photocopies of reversed tracing of same drawing	1c, 3b, 4a, 4b, 5a, 5d

Children need to have chosen their favourite drawing from the previous lesson and traced it. You will need to have photocopied both the drawing and the tracing beforehand.

Introduction
'You have been drawing patterns and shapes you found in nature. Now you are going to use one of these to create designs which could be used for fabric or wallpaper.'

Practical activity
❑ Distribute fabrics or wallpaper designs, or Resource sheet 18, to inspire children's ideas.
❑ Give out photocopies of drawings and reversed tracings.
❑ Children cut out all the drawings.
❑ Ask them to consider how they could repeat their drawings most effectively.
❑ Children arrange drawings as a pattern. They can turn some upside down, or just set them down in rows. Ask them to consider how the designs could link and repeat if they were to become a fabric or wallpaper.
❑ Once they have arrived at an arrangement they are happy with, they can stick it down.

Extension activity
❑ These designs can be photocopied (could also be reduced and more than one copy made) and then children could add colour.
❑ Here again they need to consider that the colour must also repeat in a regular way. It can look very effective if they stick to just three colours.

Background information
Photocopies and tracings are more manageable for children to use than computer drawing programs. Children find it hard to draw successfully with a mouse. The resulting drawings are often very simplified versions of the originals. With some software, drawings can be scanned and repeated, but this is time-consuming and not terribly practical for a large class.

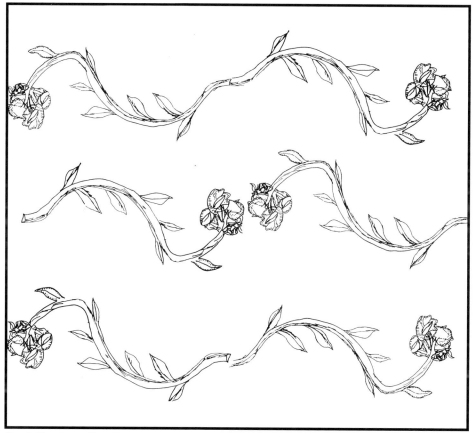

Sarah Vanstone, Year 5

71

Pattern

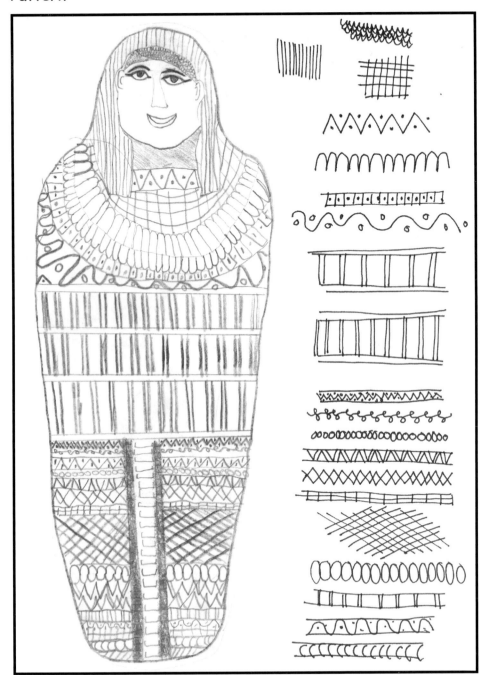

Page from Year 6 child's sketchbook

 TRY THIS IDEA!

Collecting patterns from different cultures or times

Time	Resources	National
30–40 min.	Sketchbooks	**Curriculum**
	Pencils or fine pens	1a, 1b, 4a, 4b,
	If colour notes are being made, coloured pencils	5a, 5d
	Collection of patterned artefacts or prints	
	relating to culture or periods of history being	
	studied. Could be: fabrics, weavings, pottery	
	and carvings	

Introduction

'Ideas for patterns often come from nature, like paisley in Indian designs. This is based on a leaf. Some are traditional and have been used for decoration for many years. Some are particular to one country, culture or period in history. You are going to look at these ... and draw some of the patterns that have been used.'

Practical activity

☐ Share out the objects.
☐ Children draw an artefact or part of it and label it.
☐ Next draw just the patterns from it.
☐ Children draw as many different patterns as they can find.
☐ Label them and perhaps make notes about the colours used. This could be useful if perhaps the patterns were going to be used later as a starting point for prints or a weaving.

Looking

Year 6 child's self-portrait, looking in a mirror

'The effort to see things without distortion takes something very like courage and this courage is essential to the artist who has to look at everything as though he sees it for the first time.'
Henri Matisse (from John Elderfield, The Drawings to Henri Matisse)

Why looking skills are so important

A great deal of curriculum time is given to the development of speaking and listening skills, but looking skills are overlooked. In order that drawing can be developed to the highest quality, children have to learn how to focus their whole attention on whatever it is they are drawing. Through this they will find that the longer and more concentrated the focus of attention, the more they will see.

Informed looking is very useful across the curriculum:

- ❏ In maths it develops awareness of shapes and angles, and the ability to recognize patterns
- ❏ In science it develops children's abilities to make deductions about materials
- ❏ In history children are better able to make hypotheses by looking at and handling artefacts, and by looking at historical locations and photographs
- ❏ In geography they are able to make deductions from looking at different aspects of landscapes.

Learning to draw is really a matter of learning to see. This sounds so simple. If it were simple then we would all be able to draw without needing to be taught or teach ourselves. Through learning to draw, children learn to look, and they need to look with specific intent to be able to draw well.

> 'Drawing is not really very difficult, seeing is the problem.'
> Betty Edwards,
> Drawing on the Right Side of the Brain

This chapter identifies the different skills of looking that are essential for success in drawing.

Rationale

> 'The ability to see and the ability to draw are closely related. When we are young our seeing, drawing, reading and writing develop alongside each other, but there is an emphasis in our society on literacy and the ability to comprehend mathematical concepts. As the teaching in these subjects propels us forwards, our ability to communicate in visual terms remains underdeveloped.'
> Ian Simpson, Drawing, Seeing and Observing

Learning to look carefully at the subject you are drawing is as important as, if not more important than, learning to use different media and rules about proportions. We need to help children to draw what they see, not what they think they can see. Children need help with knowing what to look for, in their subject and in their drawings, and what to do about what they see.

When the cry goes up: *'My drawing's going all wrong'*, they need to know what to do about it. If they are not given enough support there is a considerable tendency, particularly among older primary children, to give up. They rapidly gain the mistaken impression that they cannot draw.

The basic human skill which underlies drawing is the ability to make sense of the visual world, to understand it and be able to record it accurately and with sensitivity.

Precision in drawing what you see is partly a matter of practice, but the learning process can be supported and enhanced through certain checking techniques and modes of looking.

Helping children to look with new eyes

Children will often say that they can see the subject but that they cannot draw it. They become confused and feel they lack the ability, that drawing is too difficult. Children will often say they can't draw a particular subject, as in, *'I can draw dolphins but I can't draw daffodils.'* They need to be helped to understand that the drawing task ahead of them is the same whatever the subject. The key to it all is in the looking.

The most difficult task children have to overcome in drawing is that they live in a three-dimensional world which they are trying to represent on a two-dimensional surface. Three-dimensional knowledge must be re-evaluated and translated into two-dimensional shapes.

Much of learning to draw consists of discovering how things appear rather than how they are, and it is not until they begin to draw that children discover the tremendous difference between what they know and what they see. This is the old problem of drawing what you see, not what you think you see.

To help them in this difficult area, children need to be introduced to information about the left and right hemispheres of the brain and how the left and dominant side will often make it very hard for children to 'see' clearly. They need to be given drawing tasks that help exercise the right side of their brains and also help them look with fewer preconceptions and greater intensity.

Careful observational drawing is a good grounding for children, as it will enable them to draw in a more expressive way later on.

Upper Key Stage 2 children have a thirst for realism, and this needs to be accepted and met. Much as we might like them to be free from this, they are determined to have realism and feel a sense of failure if they cannot achieve it. To achieve realism they need to be able to look as an artist does. Children need strategies to help them succeed in this quest.

In Years 5 and 6 some children will want to give up, particularly boys. Boys, however, will often be more inclined to persevere with a task if they perceive it to be technical, so the lessons in this chapter are broken down into separate techniques. If children are given structured support and some tips and techniques to help them through this stage, they will realize that they can make good progress and achieve very satisfying results.

Drawing requires intense concentration. Children need to have the right learning environment to enable them to make progress in looking carefully, and drawing what they see. This requires a peaceful, quiet atmosphere, engrossing and appropriate subject matter and all the necessary materials ready to hand.

Drawing subjects that relate to children's experience, such as a pair of roller blades or a bicycle, is good for motivation and interest, but also drawing less familiar objects is excellent for creating the need for more intense looking.

What we know informs what we see or think we see. We can jump to the wrong conclusions based on a preconceived idea rather than the actual image presented to us. Children need to learn to see something as if they have never seen it before; to be unclouded by judgements about how a thing is supposed to look; to trust their eyes rather than their knowledge. Viewing the subject from unusual angles or viewpoints can help to re-focus looking.

Being able to draw well brings considerable peer approval and gives increased confidence to young artists, but they need to understand that it will involve having a serious attitude, applying themselves and persevering. It will not be easy.

About this chapter

In this chapter children will be encouraged to look in a variety of ways:

❐ Their looking will be engaged by talking about the subjects, by questioning and hypothesizing, and by touching when possible

❐ They will use focusing devices such as magnifying glasses, reflective surfaces and viewfinders

❐ They will learn about the right and left sides of the brain and how the brain affects their ability to see clearly for the purposes of drawing

❐ They will have practice in drawing and comparing shapes and judging their accuracy

❐ They will learn to see the overall shape of a subject, and start by drawing it lightly

❐ They will learn how to slow down the speed, and increase the intensity of their looking when drawing

❐ They will learn to recognize and draw right angles and parallel lines

❐ They will learn to recognize negative shapes and to understand how they can use their awareness of them to improve their own drawings

❐ They will learn the technique of sighting and how to make comparative judgements about shape and proportion.

Year 5 child's drawing of interior of classroom

List of possible subjects for drawing or discussion

Natural	**Man-made**	**Workings or insides of** (broken and/or switched off!)	**Animals**
Flowers	Carvings	Clocks	*Alive*
Leaves	Jewellery	Locks	Minibeasts
Buds	Embroidery	Circuits	Tadpoles
Seeds	Tools	Radios	Small pets
Seed heads	Kitchen tools	Televisions	Ants in ant colony
Bulbs	Kitchen equipment, e.g. egg	Computers	Worms in wormery
Sprouting beans	whisks, colanders, tin	Telephones	
Grasses	openers, etc.	Engines	*Dead*
Moss	Locks	Engine parts	Stuffed animals
Branches	Shoes	Clockwork toys	Stuffed birds
Twigs	Hats	Wheels	Stuffed fish
Bark	Umbrellas	Cogs	Mounted insects
Roots	Science equipment		Mounted butterflies
Seaweed	Pottery		
Shells	Historical artefacts		
Dried starfish	Ethnic artefacts		
Sea-horses	Toys		
Sea urchins	Rope		
Crab shells	Nets		
Wasps' nests	Gardening tools		
Pebbles	Watering cans		
Fossils	Brooms and brushes		
Feathers	Vacuum cleaners		
Nuts	Mops and buckets		
Fruit	Musical instruments		
Vegetables	Bikes		
Quartz	Roller blades		
Crystals	Rollerskates		

'For merely looking at an object cannot be of any use to us. All looking goes into observing, all observing into reflecting, all reflecting into connecting, and so one can say that with every attentive look we cast into the world we are already theorising.'
Attributed to Johann Wolfgang von Goethe

Focusing looking through talking

Time	Resources	National Curriculum
20 min.	Interesting objects that children can relate to (see list on page 77) These could be topic-led, or part of the school equipment, natural or man-made	4a

This activity can be done in relation to several other curriculum areas such as science, history or design and technology.

Introduction

'In order to draw something well you need to spend time looking carefully at it before you begin to draw. Careful looking before you start to draw will make a huge difference to your drawings. The key to drawing lies in the eyes not as you might think in the hands. You are going to be looking at, touching (if this is possible) *and talking about these objects. Later you will draw them.'*

Practical activity

Ask questions while children look at their object and think about the answer. Alternatively, pairs of children could have copies of some, or all, of the questions to ask each other.

Possible questions

❑ What overall shape is it?
❑ Is it the same shape from all sides?
❑ Can you see any right angles?
❑ Can you see any other shapes within the whole thing?
❑ Are the straight edges completely straight?
❑ Do the curved edges vary in the degree of curve?
❑ If it was photographed in black and white, what tones would there be?
❑ Is it soft or hard?
❑ What words would you use to describe the way it feels?
❑ Is it cold or warm to the touch?

❑ Do you notice any rough/smooth/shiny/sharp/spiky/fluffy parts?
❑ Is it fragile or transparent? Do any parts reflect light?
❑ Are there any broken or tattered parts?
❑ What is the widest/narrowest/thickest/thinnest part of it?
❑ What is the lightest/darkest part of it?
❑ Does it look the same if I turn it over?
❑ What is this part for?
❑ How does it join on to this bit?
❑ Does it have a smell?
❑ What does the smell remind you of?
❑ How does it sound if you tap/rattle/wind/shake/drop/spin/scrape a nail over it?
❑ What do you think it is made of?
❑ Is it all made of the same material?
❑ What angle does it join on at? Less or more than a right angle?
❑ Is it bigger than you? Me? This? That?
❑ Is it wider than it is long?
❑ Which is its widest part?
❑ Is it heavy or light?
❑ Do you think it is old or new?

Extension activity

❑ Children could take it in turns to select an artefact, take a specified length of time to look at it carefully, then describe (but not name) it from memory. Other children could ask further questions about its overall shape, textures, etc.
❑ This could be done as a whole class or in groups.
❑ Children will soon realize they have to look really carefully at the object in order to describe it to others who cannot see it.
❑ Can the class guess what it is the other child is describing?

Background information
The purpose of this activity is to involve the children with the subject, to help them see things they might not otherwise notice. Initially the describing could be done by the teacher to model the type of vocabulary and the range of observations possible.

These are some of the aspects of a subject that could be described:
- ❐ The overall shape
- ❐ Smaller shapes within the main outline
- ❐ Colours
- ❐ Textures
- ❐ Darkest and lightest areas
- ❐ Patterns
- ❐ Sounds or smells
- ❐ Comparative lengths and breadths
- ❐ Curves or angles
- ❐ Reflections
- ❐ Small details such as markings, lettering, screws, stitching
- ❐ The purpose or origin of the item
- ❐ How it was created or made, where and by whom
- ❐ How it looks from different angles.

When possible, children should have the opportunity to feel the items and describe the textures.

Year 5 child's design for playing card, based on Tudor portrait (see colour examples on front cover)

Callum Gregory, Year 6

USING SKILL Talking about the subject before drawing

Time	Resources	National
45 min. approx.	Sketchbooks Drawing media appropriate to subject matter Interesting objects that children can relate to (see list on page 77)	Curriculum 1a, 2c, 4a, 5a

Follow the pattern of focusing children's looking covered in the previous lesson. Children should have the opportunity to draw the items as soon as possible after the discussion session.

Drawing and discussion times will vary according to the complexity of the subject and the concentration levels of the children.

Introduction
'Now you have had a really close look at ... you are going to draw it. You will have at least half an hour so take your time to stop and look carefully as your drawing progresses.'

Practical activity
❏ Repeat focusing children's looking activity (pages 78–79) if you have not done it in this session.
❏ Remind children to use light lines initially.
❏ Draw the objects.

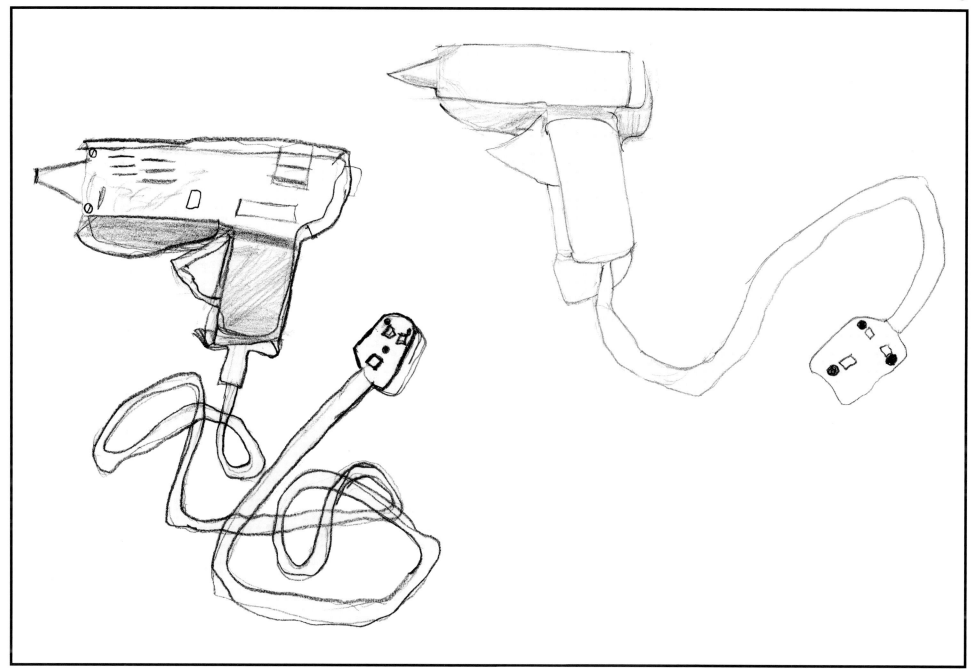

Lemar Bradford, Year 6 (close observational drawing of glue guns, see also on front cover)

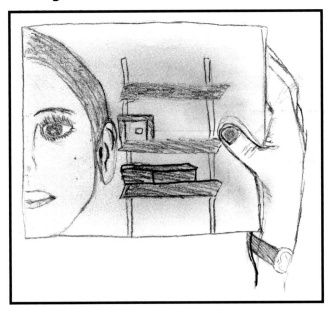

Year 6 children's drawings showing three views in one drawing: pupil's own reflection in mirror, room behind pupil in mirror and pupil's hand holding mirror

 SKILL

Using focusing devices

Time	Resources	National Curriculum
45 min. (15 min. per focusing device)	Magnifying devices: magnifying glasses (as many as you can round up); microscopes / digital microscopes / lenses Artefacts suitable for close viewing (see list on page 77) Viewfinders (see background information) Photocopy of page 85 Plastic mirrors Reflective surfaces, e.g. spoons, hub caps, any shiny metal objects	2c

Practical activities

Different devices could be used in different lessons, or there could be a carousel of activities lasting 15 minutes each.

Viewfinders

❒ Viewfinders are very useful for focusing children's looking on areas of a complex picture, in order to research the subject matter or the techniques used.

❒ The children should place the viewfinders over an area of the picture and then discuss, report or record what they see.

❒ Slide the viewfinder around and select different areas to investigate.

❒ This could be done with Bruegel's 'Children's Games' found on page 85 or pictures connected to topics being studied, such as buildings. Children could look at enlarged photographs of streets and find different tiles, doors, windows or even brick patterns.

Mirrors and other reflective surfaces

❒ Encourage children to look at themselves, then look at the background behind the reflection, and their own hand holding the mirror (see drawings on this page).

❒ They could look at a friend's reflection, noting the differences between their usual view of their friend and the reflected view.

❒ Children can stand the mirror next to an object and look at its reflection, altering the angle and noting the changes.

❏ Distorted reflective surfaces such as spoons are interesting to use. As the image is distorted, children have to look at the shapes they see rather than use prior knowledge when drawing.

Magnifying glasses, microscopes or lenses
❏ Magnifying devices are excellent for investigating the natural world in detail.
❏ Children could share items and discuss what they see now that they didn't see so well without the lenses.
❏ They could take notes and collect descriptive vocabulary.

Background information
Focusing devices help children to focus their attention on a subject or areas of a subject they might otherwise overlook. They can also help to keep children engaged in looking that little bit longer. Viewfinders are used to isolate areas of a subject and are a way of cutting out other visual information that might confuse or distract children. They can be made from stiff card or corrugated plastic. Black is best as it does not distract the eye from the subject. Cut an aperture (square, rectangular, circular, even keyhole-shaped) in the middle of the card.

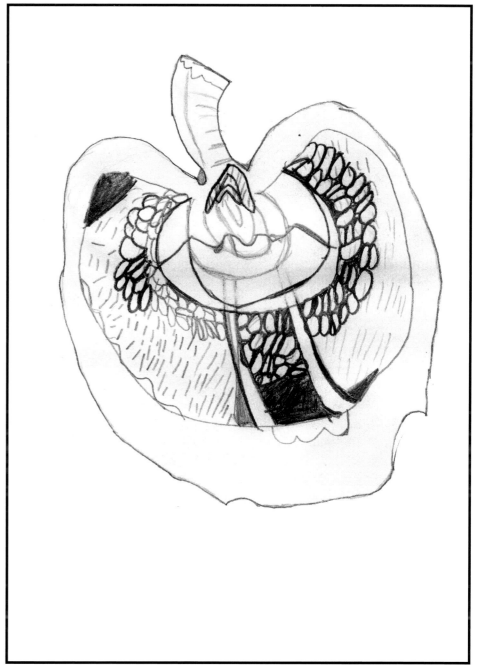

Year 5 child's drawing of the inside of a pepper, viewed through a magnifying glass

Looking

Using viewfinders to look for detail and content

Time	Resources	National Curriculum
30–40 min.	Viewfinders, one per child Photocopy of page 85 or other complex pictures Sketchbooks (if copying or recording sections of pictures)	1a, 1c, 5d

Practical activity

❐ Children could work individually or in pairs.

❐ Give each pair a complex picture to study, e.g. 'Children's Games' by Pieter Bruegel (page 85) 'V E Day' by L S Lowry or 'Portrait of a Nation' by David Mach.

❐ Ask them to lay the viewfinder over the picture and select an area that interests or attracts them. (While they are sliding the viewfinder over the picture they will come across several items they will not have noticed when looking at the whole picture.)

❐ Set a challenge: who can find, for example, a child standing on his head; someone having a piggyback ride, someone lying on a log?

❐ They can set each other challenges to find things.

❐ They could select an area and draw just that part.

❐ They could examine and record techniques the artist has used; they could search for different patterns.

❐ This is an excellent way to draw children into works of art, to show them how to look closely and with purpose.

Background information
This works quite well as a whole-class activity. Later, children could apply this process to other works of art. Textiles, embroideries, enlarged photographs of complex subject matter such as a medieval painting could all be investigated this way. David Mach's website (www.davidmach.com) is very useful for providing good pictures to study.

Detail taken from work of art on page 85

'Children's Games' by Pieter Bruegel. Reproduced with permission from Kunsthistorisches Museum, Vienna

*This page may be photocopied by the purchasing institution for their own use. © Meg Fabian, **Drawing is a Class Act, Years 5–6**, Brilliant Publications*

SKILL	# Looking for shape and form

Two- and three-dimensional shapes

Time	Resources	National Curriculum
15 min.	Artefacts that are simple and easily recognizable in terms of their shapes (two-dimensional outline shapes and three-dimensional form)	1a, 4a

Sphere/ovoid	Cuboid/cube	Cylinder
Clock – circular	Computer – square	Bottle – rectangular
Teapot – circular	Table – rectangular	Mug – rectangular
Pine cone – oval	Book – rectangular	Leg – rectangular

Introduction

'Most of the objects around us can be drawn within some simple shape. If we look at a table or chair it can be drawn within a rectangle; a bell or pear could fit into a triangle. These objects also have a "form", which is their three-dimensional shape. This same idea applies to everything around us. When you are starting to draw an object you need to look for its general shape, and then its form. Today you are going to look at some different objects. First look for the outline shape of it, then decide the form and then look for any other shapes you can see.'

Practical activity

❐ Show different objects and ask the children what overall shape they can see. Tell them to flatten the object in their mind's eye, and look at the outline.

❐ When they have decided on the object's shape ask them what form they think it is, and if there are any other shapes they can see. The outline shape will be two-dimensional but the form is three-dimensional.

❐ For example: a baked bean tin viewed from the side is a rectangle, but its form is a cylinder and it has an oval ellipse at the top. The shape of a computer might be a rectangle but the form is a cuboid and you might also see a diamond within the outline. Screwed-up paper could look round in form, but shapes within it could be triangular.

Shape and form of everyday objects found at home and at school (drawn by author)

Background information

When children learn to see things in terms of their shape they can draw anything – people, buildings, animals, landscapes. They can all be treated in the same way at the outset of the drawing. Becoming aware of the shape or shapes of the subject will be an enormous help to children to 'find a way in' to their drawings. If they think in the language of shape, the drawings they produce are more likely to resemble the reality of the things they have observed.

The three-dimensional shape of an object is known as its form.

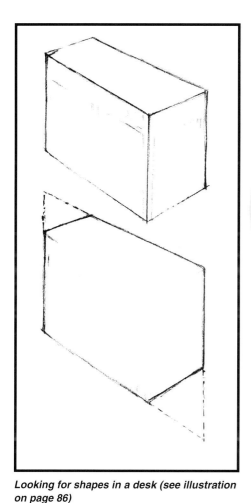

Looking for shapes in a desk (see illustration on page 86)

'The sphere the cube, the cylinder are what Cézanne called the basic forms, "all objects can be reduced to these."'
Bert Dobson,
Keys to Drawing

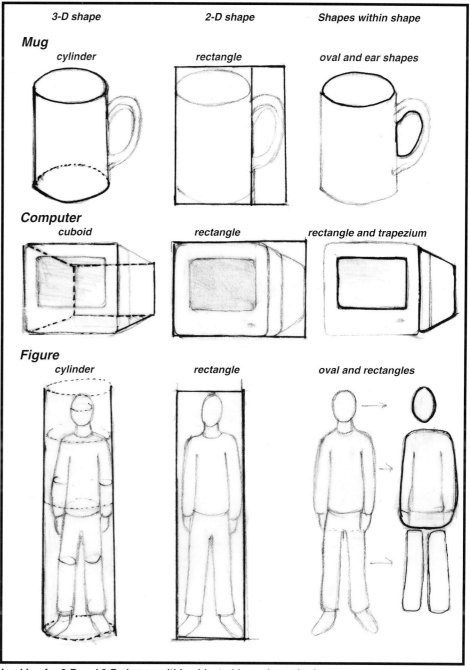

Looking for 2-D and 3-D shapes within objects (drawn by author)

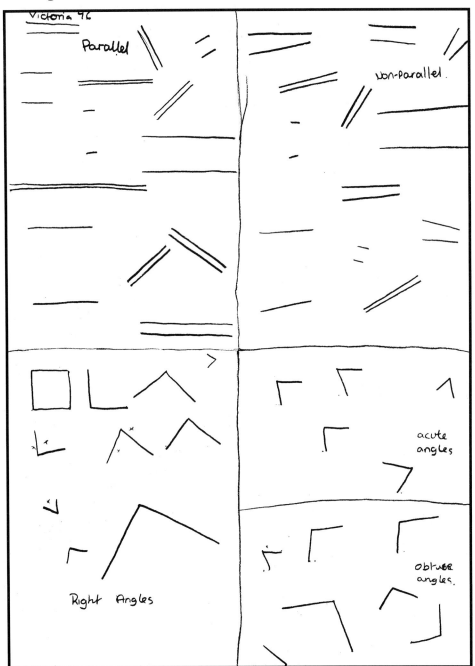

SKILL

Recognizing and drawing right angles and parallel lines

Time	Resources	National Curriculum
30 min.	Sketchbooks Any pencils Some square shapes to draw around (could also use set-squares or protractors)	4a

Introduction

'You are going to be drawing and learning to recognize different angles today. This is one of the most important skills you can acquire to help you get better at judging how well your drawings are going and, if necessary be able to put them right.'

Practical activity

☐ Revise what a right angle is.

☐ Children draw around a square, and then try drawing some lines that meet in a right angle.

☐ They can try to judge by eye if they have been successful. If not, are their angles more or less than right angles?

☐ Then they could check with a set-square, protractor or square shape and annotate their drawings.

☐ They should practise until they become reasonably competent at drawing and recognizing a right angle every time.

☐ They should then aim to draw some angles that are slightly more or less than 90 degrees, and some roughly 45 degrees.

☐ They could draw some angles for each other to check, assessing first by eye, then checking with a protractor.

☐ Next, they should try drawing pairs of parallel lines by eye (no rulers) and judge if they are parallel.

☐ Now draw pairs of non-parallel lines. Compare the two sets.

Background information
This activity only really needs to be done if children have not recently covered right angles and parallel lines in maths. It is very useful for them to be able to recognize a right angle and to judge whether another angle is more or less than it. It is equally useful for children to be able to recognize if lines are parallel or not and, if not, what angle they are to each other – opening up or converging. This ability is very important when children are judging how and where a drawing is going wrong. The ability to compare relationships between lengths, widths and angles is a key skill in drawing. That skill is covered in a separate lesson. However, children cannot make comparisons unless they can recognize angles.

Year 5 child's drawing

SKILL

Drawing geometric shapes

Time	Resources	National
30–45 min.	Pencils	Curriculum
	Sketchbooks	4a
	Resource sheet 19 (page 171)	
	Two- and three-dimensional mathematical shapes	

Practical activities

Circles and ovals

❏ Children draw round a small circle, then using a light free line go over the circle a few times.

Charlotte Green, Year 6

❏ Without the two-dimensional shape, practise drawing circles lightly and freely on the same page. Children should aim to draw very lightly with a flowing motion (teacher could model this) and try to join the circle so the line meets back at the starting point smoothly. This is easier when done quickly rather than slowly and hesitantly.

❏ Repeat this activity with an oval.

Squares and rectangles *(discourage use of rulers)*

❏ It helps if children can recognize and draw right angles and parallel lines (see previous lesson).

❏ Children draw around a square shape, looking at the angles of the corners, noting that the sides are parallel and equal.

❏ Next, without the two-dimensional shape, practise drawing squares, using light lines. Children judge by eye if they have been successful.

❏ Use same sequence with rectangles.

Cuboids and cylinders

❏ Follow Resource sheet 19 or any maths schemes or formulae the school may have for drawing three-dimensional shapes.

❏ Children may have their own formulae for drawing three-dimensional shapes and might like to demonstrate these on the board.

Background information
Before embarking on this activity it may be necessary to repeat the previous lesson (on drawing right angles and parallel lines) if children are still unable to recognize and draw these. Many of the world's greatest artists think that, if you are able to draw a sphere, a cube and a cylinder, you should be able to draw anything. If children are to be able to recognize two- and three-dimensional shapes in subjects to improve their drawings, it follows that they will need to be able to draw two- and three-dimensional shapes with reasonable accuracy or they will fall at the first hurdle. Some children will find three-dimensional shapes quite hard to draw, but explain to them that it is just a knack, and it can be picked up easily with a bit of practice. It is better that they do not use rulers but rather develop their ability to draw reasonably straight lines by hand.

USING SKILL # Drawing objects by looking for shapes

Time	Resources	National
30–45 min.	Sketchbooks	**Curriculum**
	B pencils	1a, 2b, 4a

Resources (cont.): Artefacts that have a fairly obvious overall shape, e.g. table, chair, bottles, mugs, fruit, vegetables, teapots, kettles. Enlarged Resource sheet 20 (page 172) – optional

Introduction
'Drawing shapes is easier than drawing objects, but if you can draw shapes you can draw almost anything. Seeing and then drawing the overall shape and then the smaller shapes inside is a really good way to start a drawing. This is what many of the world's greatest artists do. This is what you will be trying out today.'

Practical activity
❑ Direct the children's attention to the object they are going to draw.
❑ Ask them to identify the outline shape. Suggest they try to flatten it in their mind's eye and look at the main shape they can see.
❑ Children draw this shape lightly, filling the page.
❑ They now try to identify other shapes they can see within the outline and draw them, e.g. the curve of a label around a bottle.
❑ Draw with light lines any shapes outside the main outline, such as the handle on a mug or kettle.
❑ Suggest they note where the object is narrowest or widest.
❑ Ask if they notice any right angles or parallel or converging lines, such as the sides or legs of a table.
❑ As they notice these they should lightly draw them. Once they have the main shapes and angles they can add details, tone and darker lines.
❑ They could try as many subjects as time allows.

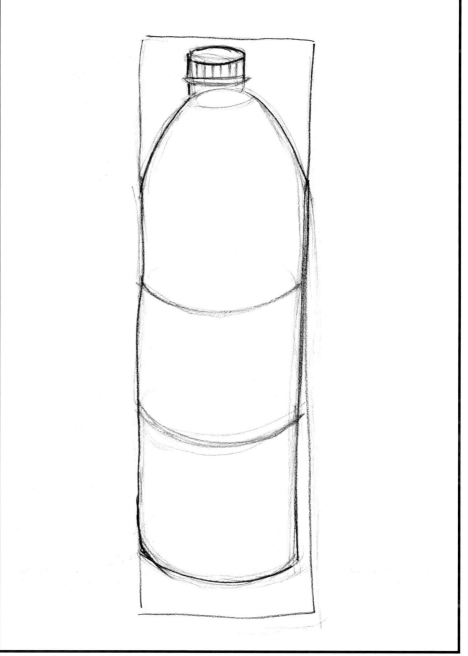
Zoe Elder, Year 5 (showing 3-D cylinder inside a 2-D rectangle)

SKILL

Sighting
Using a pencil to measure angles and comparative measurements

Time	Resources	National Curriculum
15 min.	Any full-length pencils	4a

Introduction
'You are going to learn a technique that will help you to check the different angles and proportions of whatever you are drawing. Artists use this technique to make judgements about the relative angles and sizes of things. This technique is called sighting. Using this technique you will be able to check the angle and length of one thing compared with another. When you are drawing you need to make lots of little checks as you go along to make sure you have not got anything major wrong, particularly at the beginning of the drawing.'

Practical activities
Holding the pencil
❑ Children hold a pencil out vertically in front of them with their arm fully extended (elbow locked).

Correct position for sighting

❑ They should wrap their fingers around the pencil and hold their thumb up on the side facing them.
❑ Then they should close one eye.

Checking angles
❑ Children could use the classroom as a subject.
❑ Holding the pencil as described above, children line the pencil along any vertical edge they can see.
❑ Now they can find other shapes with vertical edges by checking if the edges are at the same angle as their pencil.
❑ Then keeping their pencil at the same vertical angle, find edges of shapes that are at slightly different angles to their pencils.
❑ They should then repeat this with their pencils held out horizontally, looking for horizontal lines, then lines that are at different angles.

Checking lengths and widths
❑ Children hold pencils in the same way, still keeping arms stiff and fully extended. Closing one eye, they should line up the top of their pencil with the top of the thing they are measuring, for example the length of the window.
❑ Next they should slide their thumb down the pencil until it is in line with the bottom of whatever they are measuring.
❑ Then keeping this measurement, it can be checked against another part of the subject, or perhaps the length of another window. They can make comparisons between any widths and lengths.

Potential pitfall!
Children will think this is rather a silly activity initially, until they realize how useful it is.

Background information
Sighting is a very useful skill as it helps children see relationships between angles and lengths. *Is this bit about level? Have I got it level in my drawing? Is this at the same angle as that? Is this bit the same length as that bit? Is it about half?* It is a way of checking how accurate their drawings are, and for detecting where something may have gone wrong. Knowing what has gone wrong and what they are going to do about it gives children more control over their drawings. It only works when the subject is more than an arm's length away.

USING SKILL

Drawing using sighting
Using a pencil to measure angles and lengths

Time	Resources	National Curriculum
35–40 min.	Sketchbooks B pencils	1a, 1b, 4a

This lesson should ideally be done straight after the skill lesson 'Sighting' on the previous page. Revise the technique if some time has elapsed. It is set in the classroom, but would work anywhere.

Introduction
'You have learned about sighting and how it helps you to check the angles and measurements in your drawings. Today you are going to draw part of the classroom using sighting to check if you have got the angles and measurements about right.'

Practical activity
❏ Tell the children to look first at the part of the room they are going to draw, without sighting.
❏ Ask them to notice the vertical edges or lines they can see: sides of bookcases, doors, tables – whatever is in their field of vision.
❏ Then ask them to make a mental note of the horizontal edges and how long and wide things are compared to each other.
❏ Using sighting, now check to see if there are any angles that are not quite vertical or horizontal. Try to judge the difference between them.
❏ Children then check the comparative measurements of the main features in the room, e.g. the doors and windows.
❏ Now they map out their view using light lines (main shapes, no details).
❏ Using sighting, they check angles and comparative measurements against the ones they have drawn.
❏ Then they change anything they find to be inaccurate.
❏ Finally, they continue with their drawings, adding tone and detail.

Zoe Elder, Year 5 (drawing of window recess)

Learning to see relationships between line and shape

Time: 20 min.	Resources	National Curriculum
	Collection of small objects such as pens, pencils, books, eraser, ruler, scissors, pencil sharpener (per child)	4a

Background information
This skill will help children perceive the differences in the proportion of their subjects. If they do not see that one thing or part of a thing is wider, longer, shorter than another part, they will not draw it that way. They will tend to draw what they think is there. This is one of the most difficult habits to break in children's drawing. Directing their looking is a vital step in improving their drawing. This is also the beginning of developing the internal dialogue, that should go on while children are drawing.

Introduction
'You are going to learn to spot the difference in the sizes of objects. You will be talking to yourself in your head, asking yourself questions and looking for the answers. It will help you improve your drawing, because it will give you a way of checking if you have the shapes and sizes of things about right.

Practical activity
- ❐ Children arrange a few objects in front of them on the table; some could overlap.
- ❐ Children look at an object and compare length to width.
- ❐ Ask them to judge with their eyes what the difference is – twice as long, more than or less than twice as long? See list of questions on the following page.
- ❐ Now ask the same questions about another object in the arrangement. Tell them just to think about it.
- ❐ Now choose a third object. Ask them to compare it with the first two objects.
- ❐ Model some questions they could ask: *'How long is it compared to…? Is it longer? Twice as long? Shorter? How thick is it? Which is the thickest part? How much thicker/thinner/ wider/narrower is it than…? How much of this object is covered by that object?'*
- ❐ They could work in pairs, asking the same kinds of questions of one object compared to another.
- ❐ Explain that this is the kind of internal dialogue that should be going on during drawing.

'Exercise your eyes to see the length and breadth of things.'
Leonardo da Vinci, Treatise on Painting

Possible questions
(Using the eye to judge, not measuring)

❑ How much longer is the felt tip than the pencil? Twice as long? Less than twice as long?

❑ Which is thicker, the felt tip or the pencil?

❑ Is the eraser longer than the pencil?

❑ Which is longer? By about how much?

❑ How wide is the pencil sharpener compared to the pencil?

❑ Is the pencil sharpener closer to the eraser or the highlighter pen?

❑ Is the space between the pencil and the felt tip the same as between the highlighter pen and the fat felt tip? Which space is wider?

❑ Which object is closest to / furthest from the highlighter pen?

❑ Is the width of the highlighter pen more similar to the length of the pencil sharpener or the width of the eraser?

Children could make up their own similar questions.

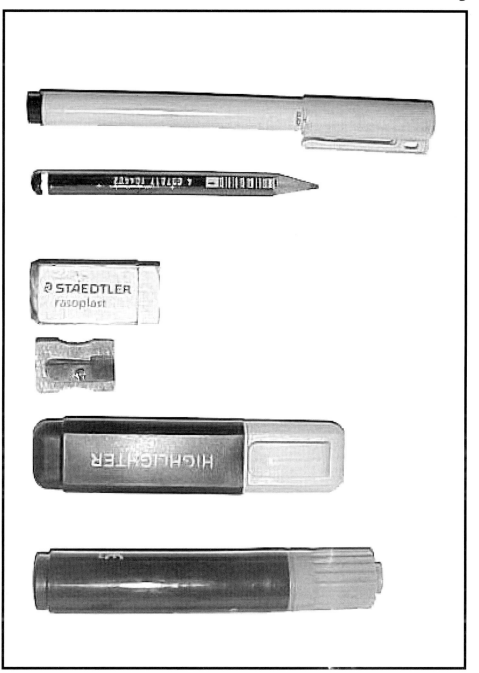

Each child should arrange his/her own collection of objects for comparison

 USING SKILL

Seeing relationships between line and shape when drawing

Time	Resources	National
30–40 min.	Sketchbooks	**Curriculum**
	B pencils	1a, 1b, 4a
	Collection of objects: books, pencils, scissors (per child)	
	Or a still life collection of objects (per group of children)	
	Copies of still life pictures	
	Resource sheets 21–22 (pages 173–174)	

This could be an opportunity to introduce still life. Examples of still life paintings (e.g. Resource sheets 21–22) could be shown to the children.

Introduction

'You have been learning the skill of judging the comparative length and width of objects, and the spaces between them. You can use this skill when drawing larger-scale subjects such as landscapes or interiors. You need to ask yourselves the same kind of questions: How wide is this wall compared to that wall? How much taller is this building/tree/hill than that one? How much wider are the windows than the door? Don't forget to look at the spaces between things as they are just as important. Whatever the subject matter, you should be asking these questions while you are drawing. You can ask them again as your drawing progresses. Look at your drawing and see if you have got the proportions about right. If not, have another look at the subject. Try to work out where you went wrong; check one measurement against another. Then alter the drawing straight away. Never put in detail or shading until you are happy that you have the main shapes about right.'

Practical activity

☐ Before starting to draw, children take a good long look at the subject.

☐ Compare lengths and widths and think about them before making any marks on the paper.

☐ When drawing a symmetrical object such as a bottle or jug, they could draw a light line down the middle of it. This will help them to judge if they have drawn both sides the same.

☐ Children should use light lines and not put in any detail or tone until the main bones of the drawing are fairly accurate.

☐ They should keep looking backwards and forwards between their drawing and the subject, checking relationships between objects. Remind them to ask themselves the kind of questions suggested on page 95 whilst looking at the spaces between objects and comparing distances. Write questions on the board for reference.

☐ Remind children to check if one object is in front of another, and if part of the object behind is hidden.

☐ Approximately half the time should be spent looking and half drawing.

Charlotte Green, Year 5

How drawing is affected by the two halves of the brain

Children usually find it very interesting to learn about the two sides of the brain.

The following two paragraphs can be read to them:

> As seen from above, your brain resembles the two halves of a walnut. These two halves are called the left and right hemispheres. The left side is dominant. It deals with knowledge, language and labelling, logic and order, numbers, time and symbols. It is the side that gets the most exercise in school.
>
> The right side is intuitive; it senses things, it makes connections but doesn't jump to conclusions, it sees likenesses between things and it deals with insight. It understands spatial relationships. The right side of the brain is one side we need to use when we are drawing.

'Learning to draw is really a matter of learning to see correctly and that means a good deal more than merely looking with the eye.'
Kimon Nicolaides, The Natural Way to Draw

How the eyes and brain work together

The eyes work in conjunction with the brain. When we look at something, we see a small upside-down image. This image is sent to the brain as coded information in the form of electrical impulses. The information is arranged in such a way that to the brain it represents the object.

No image appears in the brain. The coded information acts as a substitute for the object in the same way a word does. So in a way we see what the brain has decided we have seen. The brain is very clever at decoding the information it receives and informing us about the visual world. It uses clues in the absence of complete evidence and so can be deluded by information received and form wrong judgements – just like detectives jumping to the wrong conclusion from the facts they have gathered.

How the left side of the brain causes problems in drawing

The brain is always trying to find objects in the information it receives from the eyes and it needs very little help in order to produce them. The left side quickly names the objects and then stored knowledge steps in to complete the picture.

When the retina registers a well-known form – a tree, a house, a person or whatever – the left side of the brain immediately names it. Thereupon, children need look no further: they know all about houses and people, so the looking stops and knowledge takes over.

'As we increase the range of what we see we increase the richness of what we imagine.'
John Ruskin (from Roger Coles, Drawing with Children)

'There is only one way to learn to draw and that is a perfectly natural way. It has only to do with the act of correct observation, and by that I mean physical contact with all sorts of objects through all the senses.'
Kimon Nicolaides, The Natural Way to Draw

Children are inclined to draw from an internal model that contains central defining facts about the subject. This is why they tend to draw not what they see, but what they know and think they can see. Tree trunks are straight, no need to look, says the left side of the brain, just draw it. The trunk may actually be curved or divided, but this passes unnoticed. Taking another look seems almost like arguing with what they know. People have a head, arms, legs, feet, etc. The fact that in that particular pose the feet are hidden from view is easily overlooked. The left side of the brain knows all about people and will supply all the information, so it can cause children to draw something that they cannot see. Children draw from memorized, stored drawing symbols which are no longer appropriate to the task.

They need to learn to trust what they actually do see, to switch off the left side of the brain and let the right side take over. This is not easy, as the left side (partly because it gets so much more exercise than the right side) is dominant.

How to develop the right side of the brain

One way to develop the right side of the brain is to set a task that the left side cannot do or doesn't understand. The left side doesn't like looking at negative shapes as it can't name them, so drawing negative shapes is a good exercise.

The left side doesn't like seeing things from unusual angles as it cannot jump to conclusions so easily. Therefore, drawing things upside down is also a good exercise for the right side.

The left side dislikes drawing slowly, having to keep the eyes constantly on the subject, so children will be recording minutely what is seen but not thinking about what the object is. This is another activity which gives the right side a chance to take over. Looking and holding a mental picture of what is seen and then drawing that bit involves a shift between the left and right side, which is ideal.

The following exercises involve all these skills.

'When I eat a tomato I look at it in the same way as anyone else would, but when I paint a tomato then I see it very differently.'
Henri Matisse (from John Elderfield, The Drawings of Henri Matisse)

Examples of drawings where children have drawn the seat of a chair when they could not actually see the seat. They knew it must be there, so they drew it

TRY THIS IDEA!

How the left side of the brain causes problems

Time	Resources	National
15–20 min.	Sketchbooks Pencils	Curriculum 5a

Introduction

'As you may know, our brains have two sides – a left and right side. The left side is very good at knowing and labelling things. It is logical and ordered; it is very good at maths and language. At school it gets much more exercise than the right and so it is strong and it tends to take over whenever it can. However, it is the right side of your brain that you need to use most in drawing. The left side can make you draw things you think you see, rather than what you actually do see.'

Practical activity

❐ Place a chair on a table so that it is at eye level for the children. They should be able to see the edge of the seat but not the seat itself. *Do not draw their attention to this.*

❐ Tell them to do a quick line drawing of the chair in their sketchbooks, just the main features, no pattern or detail.

❐ A fair number of them will draw the seat, which they cannot see. Few will have drawn the underside of the seat although it could be seen. The more able children may have drawn the view correctly.

❐ While children are drawing, walk round and glance at the drawings to note how many have drawn the seat of the chair. Make no comment.

❐ Without naming names, say that some children have drawn the seat of the chair although they cannot actually see it.

❐ Explain that this is an example of how the left side of their brain has muscled in and taken over. The left side knows that a chair has a seat, four legs and a back and, because it is dominant, it takes over and tells you to draw them even if you can't see them.

- Say that the solution to this is to develop the right side of the brain, and there are exercises you can do to help.
- This can be repeated with a quick full-length figure drawing. A considerable number of children will draw a full facing view although they may well have a side view or partial side view.

'Believe what you see,
don't see what you believe.'
Meg Fabian, the author

Another example showing the seat of the chair

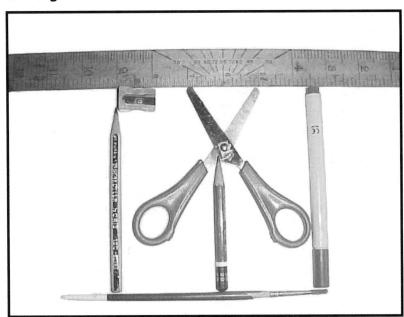

Possible arrangement of objects

Negative shapes around objects shown in photograph above

 SKILL

Seeing negative shapes

Time	Resources	National
15 min.	For each pair of children, a small collection of objects such as scissors, pencils, eraser, book, ruler	**Curriculum** 4a

Introduction

'The spaces between and around objects are just as important as the objects themselves. Objects take up a space and there is space all around them. These shapes are called negative shapes. Today you are going to start to see those shapes as shapes in their own right. Try to be aware of them from now on when you are drawing. It is another way to help you improve your drawings.'

Practical activity

❑ Get the children to place a few objects on their desks in front of them in a small group, quite close together. Some could be overlapping.

❑ Now ask them to look at the spaces between the items, to stare at them for a few moments until they can see them as shapes.

❑ Explain this is quite hard at first, but it becomes easier. They should not try to name the shapes, but try to see them as clearly as the shapes of the objects themselves.

❑ Then get the children to re-arrange the objects and look at the new negative shapes formed.

❑ Artists are always very aware of these negative shapes when they are composing a picture; they are a very important element.

❑ Lastly, put a chair up on a table where all the children can see it and ask them to see if they can see any negative spaces between the legs or around the back. This could be done with other large objects.

Background information

The ability to see negative or trapped shapes is an enormous help to children when drawing. They can use these shapes as another way of checking to see if their drawings are reasonably accurate in terms of shape and proportion. First, they need to be able to see them as shapes in their own right and as important elements of the whole subject and drawing.

USING SKILL

Seeing and drawing negative shapes

Time	Resources	National Curriculum
45 min.	Sketchbooks Sharp B or 2B pencils Resource sheet 23 (page 175) Tracing paper Large artefact, e.g. plant or chair	1a, 4a

Introduction

'You have been looking for and recognizing negative shapes. Today you are going to draw them. You should try to concentrate on them and not on the positive shapes. Negative shapes can be very big – the sky around the silhouettes of trees or buildings is a negative shape. However, today you will be drawing smaller ones.'

Practical activity

❐ Give out copies of Resource sheet 23. Ask them to lay the tracing paper on top and trace through the negative shapes only.

❐ They should then shade them in. Point out how, by drawing just the negative shapes, they have also drawn the objects. This will help them understand that both sets of shapes are important.

❐ Draw their attention to negative shapes in the classroom: the spaces between chair legs, around display boards, etc.

❐ Place the object to be drawn where it can be viewed to advantage. Remind them to look only at the negative shapes.

❐ Allow plenty of time for the children to look at them before they start to draw. Remind them that when they draw in future they will be looking at and drawing both sets of shapes.

❐ At the end of the activity they could shade in the negative shapes so they stand out.

Background information

The spaces in, around and between objects are generally referred to as negative shapes. Children often ignore them when drawing, but they are as important as the shapes themselves. They are an important element in composition and children can use them to check the accuracy of the shapes and proportions in their drawings. This should be stressed or they may not take the activity seriously.

Daisy Perham, Year 6

103

Correct drawing position for activity

 SKILL

Slowing down the speed of looking
Drawing without looking at the paper

Time	Resources	National
20–30 min.	Sketchbooks HB pencils	Curriculum 5a

This exercise involves very intense concentration as it is a kind of looking the children may never have done before. If they are concentrating intently, a deep silence falls on the class and the temperature in the room rises perceptibly. It is quite a good idea to open a window to allow more oxygen in. Some children may complain that their head aches a little. Tell them this is because they are using a part of their brain that doesn't get as much exercise as the other parts, and like an unused muscle it aches when used.

Introduction

'Sometimes when drawings seem to be going wrong it could be because you are drawing and looking at different speeds. Perhaps your hand is moving to draw before your eye has even seen. Today you will be doing a job the left side of the brain can't do, so the right side gets a chance to be exercised. It will help you to look very closely. You don't have to worry how the drawing will turn out. It will look very strange, but that doesn't matter. What matters today is how closely you look.'

Practical activity
Setting up

☐ Children need to sit so that their pencil is poised over their paper but their bodies and knees and heads are completely turned away.

☐ Left-handed children will be facing the opposite direction to right-handers.

☐ The outline of the children's non-drawing hand is the subject.

❐ Children fix their eyes on any point on their hand and let their eyes travel very, very slowly around the outside edge of it, taking in every minute detail, every tiny change in contour. Their eyes must be like a super-efficient machine tracking and scanning. They must move very, very slowly.

Drawing

❐ Once they have really slowed down their speed of looking they should start to draw, *without looking at the paper*, exactly what their eyes see. Their pencil should draw at exactly the same speed as their eyes travel.

❐ Tell them to imagine there is a direct connection between their eyes and their pencil. As their eyes see something, their pencil draws it at the exact same moment. Explain that it does not matter what the drawing looks like and not to worry about it – it will look strange.

❐ Five minutes may be all they can manage the first time this is done, but when they have had a short break they should draw again for a little longer, perhaps drawing a whole figure using a model.

Potential pitfall!

Children may try to rush this first time, thinking it is easy, and just draw a hand from memory. Emphasize the slowness.

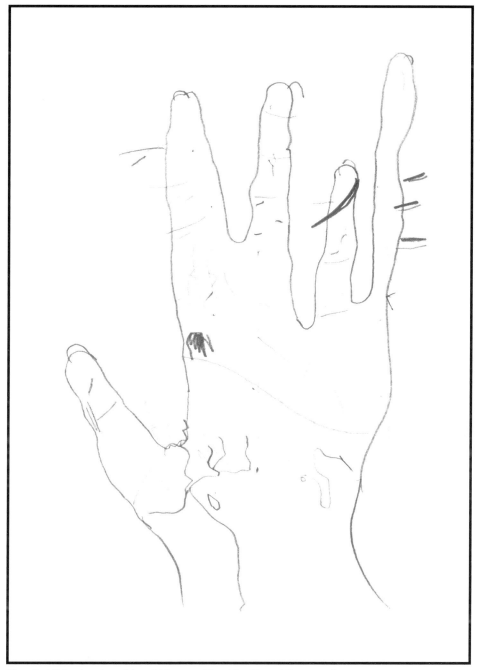

Year 6 child's drawing of hand (drawn without looking at the paper)

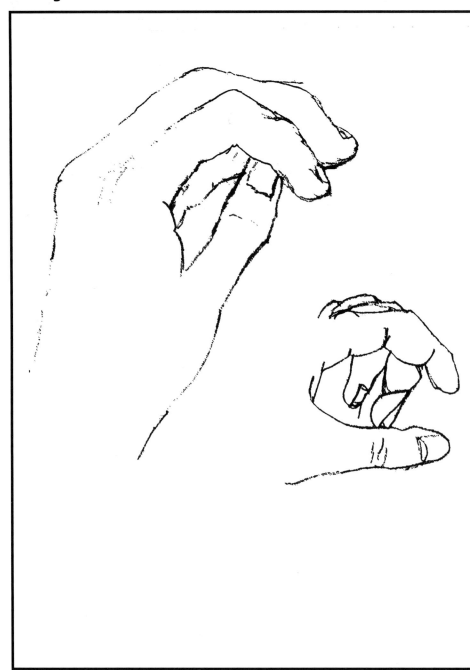

Year 6 child's closely observed drawing of own hand

 USING SKILL

Looking and drawing very slowly

Time	Resources	National
20 min.	Sketchbooks	Curriculum
	HB or B pencils	4a

Introduction
'You are going to exercise the right side of your brain today. You will be drawing one of your hands again and you will still be turned away from the paper but this time you can occasionally glance down just to check where your pencil is. The main focus of this lesson is to concentrate on looking. When you are drawing, don't think in terms of fingers or nails, just think of the shapes and lines. If you think about what things are, the left side of the brain will take over and tell you what you should draw, then you will be drawing what you know, rather than what you can see.'

Practical activity
❒ Children sit in the same position as in the previous lesson.
❒ They could put the hand they are going to draw in a different position from the last lesson. A half-closed fist is good but they should rest their hands or wrists on the table as this pose will take longer and may be hard to hold.
❒ Ask children to decide where they will start to look on their hand. Place the pencil point on the paper and start to draw very slowly as their eyes travel slowly around the outside edge of their hand.
❒ Tell them to include every tiny change of angle, lump, bump, wrinkle or fold they see.
❒ They can occasionally glance down at the paper just to check where they are on the page.
❒ After 5–10 minutes they could include some internal lines or marks.

Potential pitfall!
Sometimes it is difficult to settle children down to this activity. They might think it is just plain silly. That is why it is a good idea to explain to them about the left and right side of the brain (see pages 98–99). Unfortunately, they may still think it is silly.

Background information
This is a few steps away from pure contour drawing, where children do not look at the paper at all, and a few steps nearer the ideal looking/drawing ratio, which is 50/50. In this exercise children will still be looking and drawing much more slowly than usual. It is useful to draw children's attention to the contrast between how much time they spend looking at the subject in this lesson compared to the length of time they would have spent previously. Children often spend as little as 10 per cent of their drawing time actually looking.

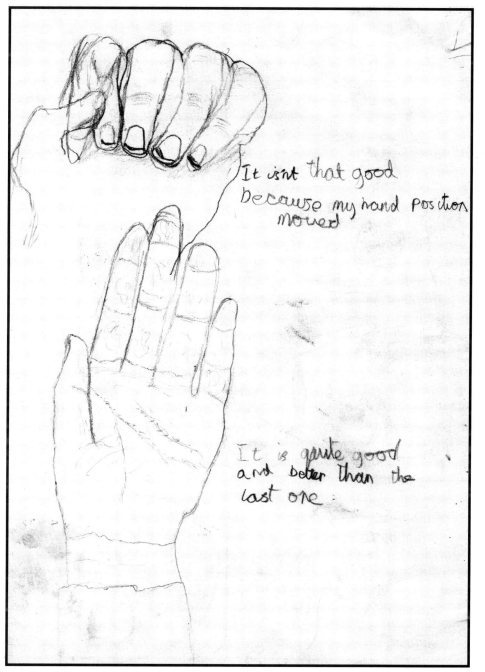

Year 5 child's page from sketchbook

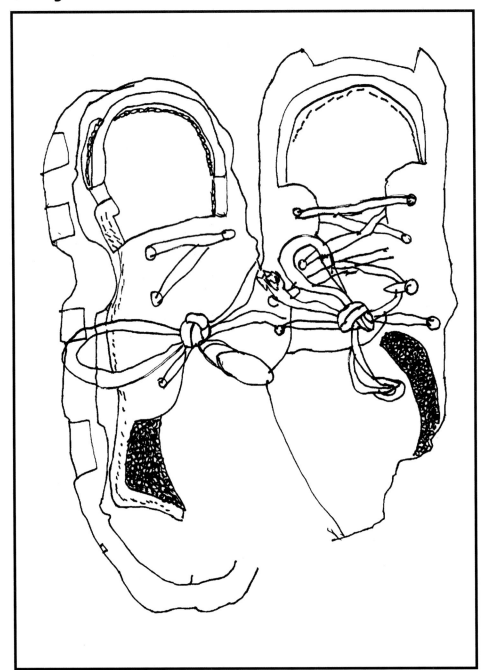

Oliver Vanstone, Year 5

| SKILL | **Looking, holding, drawing a line** |

Time	Resources	National
20 min.	Sketchbooks	Curriculum
	HB or B pencils	4a, 5a

In this lesson children will be developing the skill of looking, taking note of a small part of the subject, holding it in their minds for a moment, and then drawing it while the image is still fresh in their memory.

Introduction
'This drawing activity will help you to use the right and left sides of your brain together. You will be looking, memorizing what you see, and then drawing. You will only need to look at and memorize a small part of the subject at a time. Notice that you are not being asked to think about what it is that you are drawing. You don't want to give the left side of your brain a chance to take over. You will just be thinking about lines and shapes.'

Practical activity
- ❐ Children sit with their sketchbooks on their laps, their ankles crossed and with a clear view of their legs straight out in front of them.
- ❐ They will be drawing their crossed feet.
- ❐ Explain that they are going to use a look/hold/draw process.
- ❐ This means looking hard, taking a note of part of the outline, holding it in their memory, drawing it, then looking at the next part, holding it, drawing it. A natural rhythm should develop.
- ❐ They should try to leave their pencil point on the paper while they are looking and memorizing.
- ❐ When the outline shape is drawn, they can look at and draw intersecting lines and details.
- ❐ Warn them not to think *'This is the shoe lace'* or *'This is the sole'* as naming things gives the left side a chance to take over and dictate what is to be drawn. Just look at lines and shapes.

Background information

All drawing, unless it is pure contour drawing (i.e. not looking at the paper), is drawing from memory. It consists of looking at the subject, taking a mental picture, holding the picture in the memory and then looking down at the paper and drawing. This activity exercises the brain to shift between left and right modes. It is in the interaction between left brain logic and right brain creativity that the greatest learning and understanding takes place.

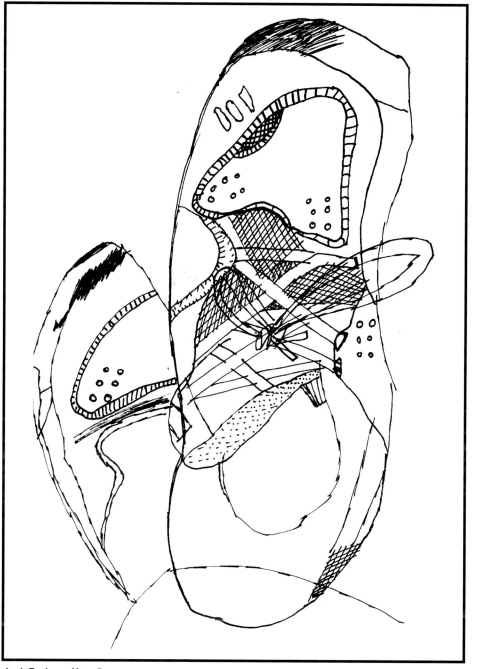

Jack Perham, Year 5

Drawing upside down

Time	Resources	National Curriculum
30 min.	Sketchbooks HB or B pencils Resource sheet 24 (page 176)	4a

It can help children draw what they see rather than what they think they can see if they draw from unusual viewpoints. The purpose of this lesson is to demonstrate how they should always try to look with fresh eyes and forget what they know about something. Children unintentionally refuse to see the true shapes and sizes of things because they have preconceived ideas about them. This is how the left side of the brain can cause problems in drawing. In this activity it is difficult for the left side of the brain to interpret what is seen, and so the right side is able to take over.

Introduction

'Today you are going to be copying a drawing, but some of you will be drawing it upside down! Don't worry about what the drawing is, just concentrate on the shapes, lines and angles that you see. In some ways it is easier to copy the drawing when it is upside down than to copy it the right way up. We will compare the two sets of drawings at the end of the lesson.'

Practical activity

❒ Give half of the class (the younger or less able children) the photocopies of Resource sheet 24, placed upside down in front of them and tell them not to turn them the right way up.

❒ Tell them to start copying from the bottom of the drawing (this is in order to concentrate their attention on lines and shapes rather than on a face).

❒ Discourage any discussion about the subject matter of the drawing.

❒ The other half of the class can have the drawing the right way up and start where they like. They have the harder job. Tell them this, but they won't believe you!

❒ They should all use as many of their looking strategies as they can. For example, look for:
  * The halfway point in the drawing
  * How long or short one line or shape is compared to another
  * The shapes between other shapes
  * The distances and angles between lines
  * How far along each side of the frame of the picture the intersecting lines come.

❒ Children should keep looking at the picture and their own drawing, looking and checking continually. Look to see how and where and at what angle one line or shape joins onto another.

❒ They should try not to name parts of the drawing, such as the nose or an eye. This would give the left side a chance to take over and the intense looking will stop. Explain that the finished drawing is not the most important thing: it is the analytical looking that matters most.

❒ Compare the two sets of drawings. The upside down group will most probably have made a surprisingly good job.

❒ Explain that it is because they were looking at lines and shapes rather than thinking about what it was they were drawing. The left side of their brain wasn't allowed to dominate.

Keep the paper this way up.

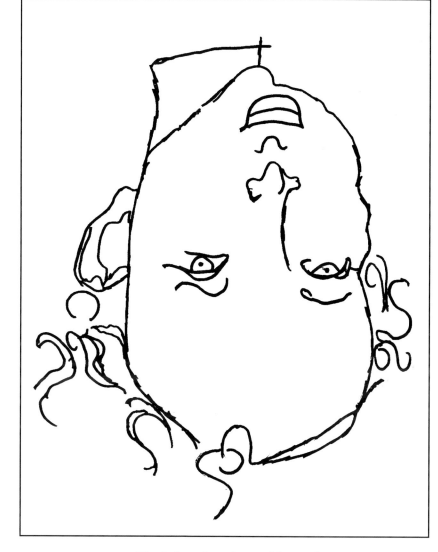

'Head of Child' by Henri Gaudier-Brezska (reproduced with permission from Tate, London 2005)

Start drawing from this end.

Resource sheet 24 completed by Stephen Grimshire (picture drawn upside down)

Looking strategies children could use when drawing

1. Looking for the main shapes

2. Looking for shapes within shapes

3. Looking for parallel lines

4. Looking for right angles

5. Looking for negative shapes

6. Sighting to check angles

7. Looking at comparative lengths and widths

8. Looking and drawing more slowly

9. Looking for longer before drawing

10. Trusting what you see, not what you know

Self-assessment of looking strategies

Did you use any of the following strategies when you were drawing?

❏ Looking for the main shapes .... Yes / No

❏ Looking for shapes within shapes .... Yes / No

❏ Looking for parallel lines .... Yes / No

❏ Looking for right angles .... Yes / No

❏ Looking for negative shapes .... Yes / No

❏ Sighting to check angles .... Yes / No

❏ Looking at comparative lengths and widths .... Yes / No

❏ Looking and drawing more slowly .... Yes / No

❏ Looking for longer before drawing .... Yes / No

❏ Using light lines at the start of the drawing .... Yes / No

❏ Which strategies helped the most? (put the numbers from list on left)

❏ Do you need to go over any of them again? .... Yes / No

❏ Which ones?

❏ What would you like to get better at in drawing?

Figures and faces

Heidi Green, Year 5

Year 5 child's drawing showing face divisions

Rationale

One of the most important aspects of school life is the adults and children who make up the school community. Therefore what could be more useful or relevant to children in drawing than to be able to draw people?

Drawing people (figure drawing) is a fundamental part of art education. Children are quite likely to be asked to include people in illustrations across the curriculum. That probably means being able to do it from memory. They need to be able to draw figures with fairly accurate proportions, quickly and easily. To do this they need to be taught a few basic rules, and they need practice.

Drawing people is like drawing anything else in so much as you need to look hard at the subject.

Potential pitfalls!

Here are some common problems that crop up almost universally when children draw faces and figures:
- ❒ Heads tend to be too big
- ❒ Eyes are too near the top of the head
- ❒ Necks are missing or too narrow
- ❒ Shoulders are too narrow
- ❒ Arms are too short
- ❒ Feet are too small
- ❒ Both feet point the same way or
- ❒ Feet are at a 180-degree angle to each other.

Basic rules

Here are some simple pointers about average body proportions and shapes. These are only intended as a starting point, not a formula. Photocopiable versions of these pointers appear on Resource sheets 25 and 26 (pages 177 and 178).

Shapes and proportions in figure drawing
Body shapes and lengths and leg lengths vary enormously but generally:
- ❒ You can fit about 5–6 heads into a child's body (6–7 into an adult's body).
- ❒ Arms, legs and necks are cylinders.
- ❒ Legs start just below halfway line.
- ❒ Arms end on halfway line, hands come below.
- ❒ Arms fit into shoulders just as sleeves into a jacket.
- ❒ Shoulder to elbow and elbow to wrist are equal lengths.
- ❒ Shoulders are twice as wide as the width of the face.
- ❒ Shoulders slope slightly.
- ❒ Necks are slightly narrower than heads.
- ❒ Foot length is similar to head length.

Useful points for action poses:
- ❒ The torso is divided into two equal parts: shoulder to waist and waist to top of thigh.
- ❒ During action poses these parts can be at different angles to each other.

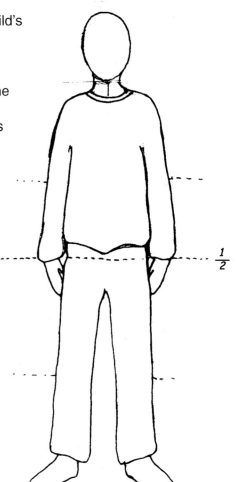

$\frac{1}{2}$

Shapes and proportions for facial features
- ❐ From the front, heads are roughly oval.
- ❐ The neck is a cylinder.
- ❐ Faces vary in shape; some are more square, some more pointed, some more rounded.
- ❐ Eyes are half way down the face.
- ❐ Eyes are roughly one eye-width apart.
- ❐ Eyes are almond shaped but eyeballs are spheres.
- ❐ Eyelids cover this shape and are therefore curved.
- ❐ Eyelids have a thickness; there is a shadow above and below.
- ❐ Eyelashes do not radiate out from lids like rays of the sun.
- ❐ You can rarely see the whole iris.
- ❐ The pupils are in line with the corners of the mouth.
- ❐ The mouth is roughly half way between the base of the nose and the chin.
- ❐ The line between the lips is the darkest.
- ❐ The top lip is often in shadow and so darker than the lower lip.
- ❐ The inner corner of the eye is in line with the nostrils.
- ❐ Ear tips are roughly level with eyebrows, bottoms level with the tip of the nose.
- ❐ The hairline starts below the top of the head (unless the model is balding!).

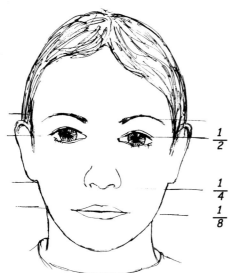

About this chapter

By Years 5 and 6 children are more and more concerned with realism. We might not want them to be, but they are, and they can be easily discouraged when their drawings don't meet their aspirations. It is at this stage many children give up, particularly boys. The cry goes up: *'I'm rubbish at drawing. This is too difficult. It keeps going wrong.'* Perhaps because other children can see their efforts, they feel self-conscious and concerned about peer pressure and fears of ridicule.

This chapter supports their quest for more realism in face and figure drawing through a variety of approaches.

In this chapter they will:
- ❐ Be given guidelines and a framework for drawing faces and bodies
- ❐ Draw active poses from life and from memory
- ❐ Develop an awareness of outline and internal shapes
- ❐ Study individual facial features in detail
- ❐ Use mirrors to draw self-portraits
- ❐ Use all these skills while completing a longer pose
- ❐ Evaluate their drawings and identify what they might change in future work.

Year 5 child's drawing (10 minute pose)

 KEY SKILL

Drawing the whole body
A simple standing pose

Time	Resources	National
45 min.	Sketchbooks	**Curriculum**
	B pencils	1a, 1b, 3a, 3b
	Resource sheet 25 (page 177)	

A very useful drawing skill is that of making comparative shape and size judgements: *How much longer/shorter/wider/narrower is this line/shape than that?*

In figure drawing, that would mean asking such questions as:
❑ How much wider are the shoulders than the hips?
❑ What is the difference between the length of the legs and the body?

Children should look at the model, back at the drawing, check the model again, then make any necessary changes. They should not draw facial features, nor detail on clothes. The focus is the whole-body shape and proportions.

The pose should be a simple standing one, with arms by the sides. The teacher could be the model – that way no child misses this initial lesson. It is useful to watch them drawing and note how often they look at you. It should be 50% looking and 50% drawing.

Figure drawing skills will improve greatly with practice. The more often this lesson is done, the greater the progress.

Introduction
'Today you will be drawing the head and body; artists call this figure or life drawing. You can check your drawings against these guidelines (show Resource sheet 25) *for average body proportions.'*

Practical activity

☐ Discuss the body proportion guidelines (Resource sheet 25).
☐ Children should draw a light straight vertical line where they plan to draw the figure. Proportions can be marked off along this.
☐ Next mark the halfway point.
☐ Children now have 10 minutes to draw the whole figure. Stress that they must draw the whole figure from head to feet. No detail should be added at this stage.
☐ Draw the head and neck, making a light oval which takes up about an eighth of the line (a sixth in a child). The bottom of the line will be for the feet. The halfway point is roughly where the legs start.
☐ Shoulders should be sketched in next (check width compared to head), then arms, ending at about the halfway mark, hands below this.
☐ Children can now add the rest of the figure, legs, feet, clothes.
☐ Ask children to think what they will improve in their next drawing.
☐ Repeat the activity as often as you have time for.

One set of these drawings from each child could be kept as part of their records of development (see page 148).

Potential pitfall!

Children tend to get bogged down in drawing facial features, which does not leave them enough time to draw the whole figure or check body proportions.

Felicity Cook, Year 6

117

KEY SKILL
Drawing different poses

Time	Resources	National Curriculum
40 min.	Sketchbook	
(10 min.	2B or B pencils	1a, 1b, 3a, 3b,
each pose)	Resource sheet 25 (page 177)	5a

When pupils are confident about drawing simple standing poses, they can transfer their skills to the drawing of more complex poses. Models could be different pupils for each pose, unless an adult can be persuaded. Allow 10 minutes for each pose. Do as many as you have time for.

Practical activity
❐ Set up a simple pose initially – it will be easier for the children to remember and check body proportions (referring back to the sheet).
❐ Children draw a light line first and mark off top, bottom and halfway points.
❐ Start drawing from the head, leaving out facial features and details. Check how many heads fit into the body and make it bigger or smaller if necessary before going any further.
❐ When main body proportions are fairly accurate, add features, detail and some tones and textures.
❐ Use the model breaks for evaluation. Children can think about how they will improve and develop their next drawings.
❐ In subsequent poses, try different arm and leg positions, with the weight unevenly distributed. When the pose is set, ask the children first to look at the overall shape of the figure and then to note the angles of hip and shoulder lines. These may not be horizontal as they were in the simple pose.
❐ Try poses with a prop, e.g. a racket and ball.

Potential pitfall!
Seated poses can be quite challenging due to foreshortening. Children will need to compare lengths and shapes within the pose to judge the foreshortened measurements, e.g. how long the foreshortened thigh is compared to the length of the lower leg.

Contour figure drawing

SKILL

Slowly drawing the outline of the figure without looking at the paper

Time	Resources	National Curriculum
30 min. (5 min. per drawing)	Sketchbooks B or 2B pencils	1a, 1c, 2b, 4a

Introduction

'Today you are going to try out a new drawing technique. It is called contour drawing. Your drawings may not look much like figures to begin with, but you will be getting better at looking and drawing only what you can see. Looking carefully is an important skill for people in many occupations – for example scientists, historians, geographers, actors – as well as artists.'

Practical activity

❒ Children will be drawing the figure's outline without looking at the paper.

❒ They should decide where on the outline of the figure to start looking.

❒ As their eyes travel very slowly around the outside of the figure their pencils must draw exactly what their eyes see at exactly that moment. They need to imagine their eyes are giving a message directly to their pencil.

❒ The slower their eyes travel, the more they will see and the easier it is to draw accurately.

❒ Children will be highly amused by their efforts initially. However, this exercise actually requires intense concentration.

❒ When a few contour drawings have been completed, allow children to glance down occasionally as they do the next set of drawings. They can briefly check their progress and add internal lines.

Warning

The resulting drawings will cause much hilarity when children see them!

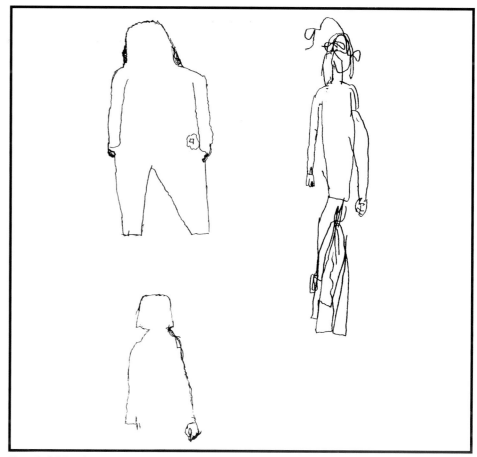

Year 5 children's contour drawings (drawn without looking at the paper)

Background information

This is an exercise that should be done slowly. A contour drawing does not have to be finished; it is an experience than takes as long as children have the patience to look. They do not need to worry about the proportions of the figure or the look of the drawing; it is the intensity of the looking at the subject that is paramount. A contour drawing should be done without looking down at the paper. Children will find this very hard at first and may look down without realizing. They should draw the outline of the figure very slowly as their eyes travel slowly over the subject, and the pencil draws exactly what the eyes see. The exercise will need to be explained carefully to the children as they will find it rather strange at first. First attempts may only take a few moments; as they begin to understand the exercise they will take longer.

119

Examples of very quick, one minute drawings

 SKILL

Gesture figure drawing
Sketches of action poses

Time	Resources	National Curriculum
30 min.	Sketchbooks 4B pencils, graphite, Conté crayons (soft pastels) or charcoal (any drawing medium for fast, flowing drawing)	1a, 1c, 2b, 4a

These sketches try to catch the feeling of the pose, what the model is doing rather than how they actually look. The drawings are done very quickly, less than a minute for each. Children should draw rapidly using continuous line, without taking the pencil off the paper, recording the gesture. They will be glancing back and forth continually between model and paper. All the poses should be very active: throwing a ball, reaching down or up, crouching as if ready to sprint. Sketching could be done during a PE lesson, in the playground, or of animals or small children.

Introduction
'Sometimes we want to draw an action pose, when the action or gesture is the most important thing about the drawings. Today we are going to try and catch the 'feeling' of the pose, and to imagine how the model actually feels as they bend or stretch, muscles pulling, back aching. Quick sketching will help keep our drawing skills sharp.'

Practical activity
❑ Revise information on body proportions (see page 114).
❑ Set up a simple action pose, which can be held for one minute.
❑ Tell children to try to capture the feeling of the pose.
❑ Children have one minute to draw the figure, the pencil travelling quickly over the paper in a continuous line.
❑ They should draw the main shapes, lines and gist of the pose: the arched back, the arms flung outwards or the bent lines of the legs.
❑ Lines will be drawn over other lines in rapid succession.
❑ Explain that artists often have to record what they see very quickly before the scene changes, so this is a very useful skill to develop.
❑ Do as many different poses as you have time for.

SKILL

Figure drawing from memory
Seeing the figure as a whole shape

Time	Resources	National
30 min.	Sketchbooks	Curriculum
	4B pencils, graphite, Conté crayons (soft pastels)	1a, 1c, 2c
	or charcoal (any drawing medium suitable	
	for fast, flowing drawing)	

Introduction

'Today you will be drawing a model from memory. You will have a few moments to look at the pose, and then you will have to quickly draw what you have seen. Try to see the figure as a whole shape.'

Practical activity

❏ Ask the model (it could be you) to take a pose and hold it for about half a minute.

❏ During this time describe how the model is posing, e.g. arms are crossed, head is slightly to one side.

❏ Children look, but do not draw.

❏ Explain that the most important piece of equipment they have for drawing is their eyes. Tell them to be like a camera; take in the whole picture, like a mental snapshot.

❏ When the model steps down, the children have a minute or so to quickly draw what they remember. They should draw the whole figure, the main lines and shapes, but no details.

❏ Repeat this activity with different poses each time.

Background information

When drawing completely from memory children need to remember the whole figure, the overall shape and mood of the pose. Most drawing, with the exception of contour drawing, involves some memory. When children are looking back and forth between the model and the paper, what they are doing is memorizing little bits at a time. This exercise is good training as it helps them to see the figure as a whole shape.

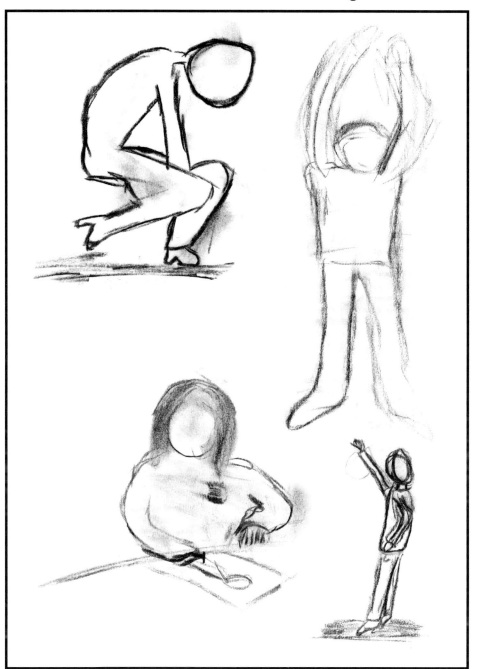

Drawing from memory – two minute drawings

Becky Jewel, Year 6

 SKILL # Drawing heads and position of features

Time	Resources	National Curriculum
30 min.	Sketchbooks B or 2B pencils Mirrors Resource sheet 26 (page 178)	1a, 1c, 4a, 5a

Children tend to make inaccuracies when drawing heads and faces. The eyes are drawn too high, necks tend to be too narrow and the hairline starts too high up the head. Getting proportions correct in portraits helps children to achieve a likeness. It might be useful for children to have a copy of Resource sheet 26 stuck in their sketchbooks as a reference.

Introduction
'Today you are going to draw heads and faces; you will be looking at where the features come on the face and how the hair grows. If you want to make your portrait look like the sitter, it is important to get the position of features and shapes and proportions as near right as possible. People vary enormously but there are some general rules that are useful to remember when drawing portraits.'

Practical activity
❐ Read the guidelines together (Resource sheet 26) and give out the mirrors.
❐ Explain that although head and face shapes vary they are mostly oval. Say, *'Think rugby ball, not football'*.
❐ Children should draw a large oval lightly, adjusting the shape of the face later if necessary.
❐ Divide the oval in half vertically. This line is useful to check symmetry.

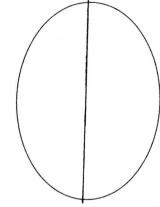

❏ Divide face in half horizontally. Draw eyes on this line, about one eye-width apart. Draw eyebrows above, checking the shape in the mirror. (Note: Year 6 children should draw the horizontal lines slightly curved, as the lines are travelling across the ovoid shape of the head.)

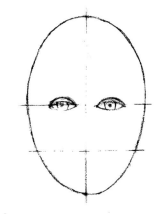

❏ Divide the lower half in half again horizontally. Look in the mirror. Draw nostrils along this line.

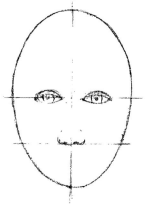

❏ Divide the lower quarter in half, horizontally. Look in the mirror. Draw the mouth along this line, with the mouth corners vertically in line with the pupils.

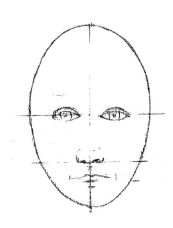

❏ Draw ears (if visible), tips level with eyebrows, lobes level with the nostrils.

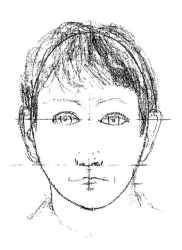

❏ Point out how the hairline starts below the top of the head.
❏ Children look in the mirror at how their hair grows: down the forehead in a fringe, combed to the side or back. Ask how far down the side of the head it comes, whether it covers the ears, and so on. Draw in the hair.
❏ Now change the face shape if necessary, adding a few character details.
❏ Lastly draw the neck, starting below the earlobes.

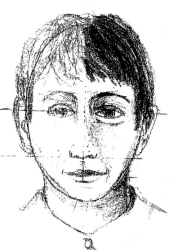

Muscle tone and extra detail have been added to the right hand side of this face.

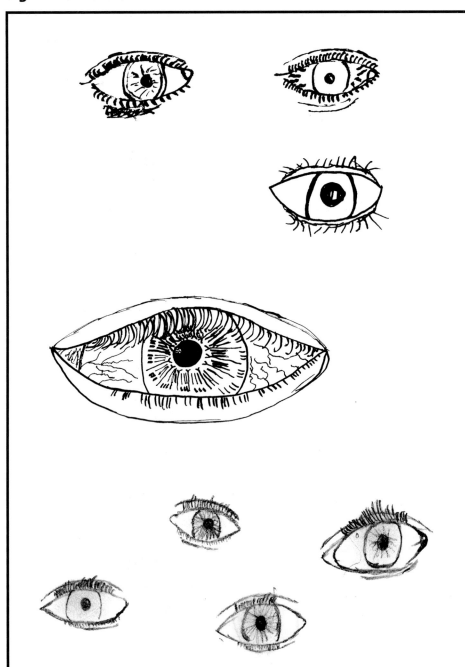

Years 5 and 6 children's drawings of eyes

 SKILL

Drawing eyes

Time	Resources	National
30 min. approx.	Sketchbooks B or 2B pencils Mirrors Resource sheet 26 (page 178)	Curriculum 1a, 1b, 2b, 5a

Introduction
'Having worked on the positions of the features, you are going to spend more time drawing and looking at them very carefully, using mirrors and looking at each other. Today you will be drawing eyes, sometimes referred to as "the mirrors of the soul". If you can get the eyes looking lifelike and in the correct position, you are well on the way to creating a good likeness in a portrait.'

Practical activity
❒ Children look in the mirror and talk about the shape and colour of their eyes and eyelashes, comparing them with whoever is sitting nearest.

❒ As a class, read the notes about eyes, eyelids and lashes (Resource sheet 26). Children could check these against their own eyes.

❒ Ask them to look at the lower eyelashes and see how they differ from the upper lashes. Explain that it is this kind of detail that will give their self-portraits character and likeness.

❒ Ask them to look at how the lashes grow out of the upper and lower lids.

❒ Next look carefully at the iris and notice the lines radiating from the pupil and the reflected light near the middle.

❒ Draw their attention to the shape of the whites and the corners of their eyes. Remind them that you can rarely see the whole iris.

❒ Now they could draw their own eyes, remembering to include all the things they have noticed.

❒ They could also add shadows and lines beneath the eyes, if they have any.

- ❏ Discuss with children the variety of shapes to be found in eyebrows, e.g. arched, straight, thick, fine, meeting across the bridge of the nose.
- ❏ Children should look at the shapes of their eyebrows and the distance between them and their eyes. If they compare their eyebrow shapes and positions with a partner's it will help them to recognize how different they can be.
- ❏ Finally tone can be added.

Background information

Children tend to have developed schema for drawing facial features. This lesson encourages them to have another look at the shapes and to draw what they see rather than what they think they know about them. Profiles are more difficult than full-face portraits, and are briefly covered on pages 130–131.

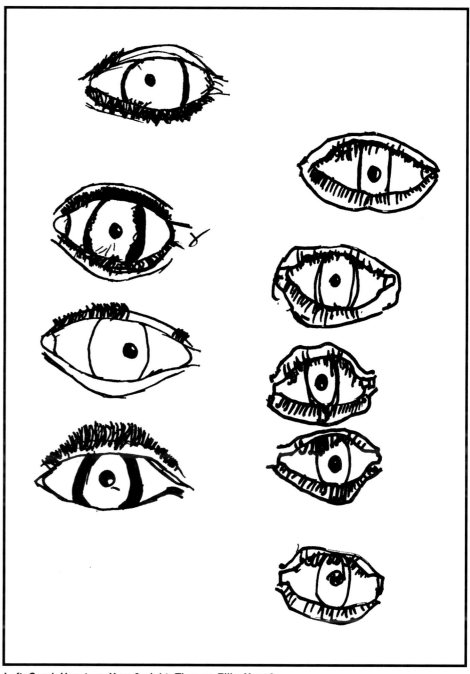

Left: Sarah Vanstone Year 6; right: Thomas Ellis, Year 6

Figures and faces

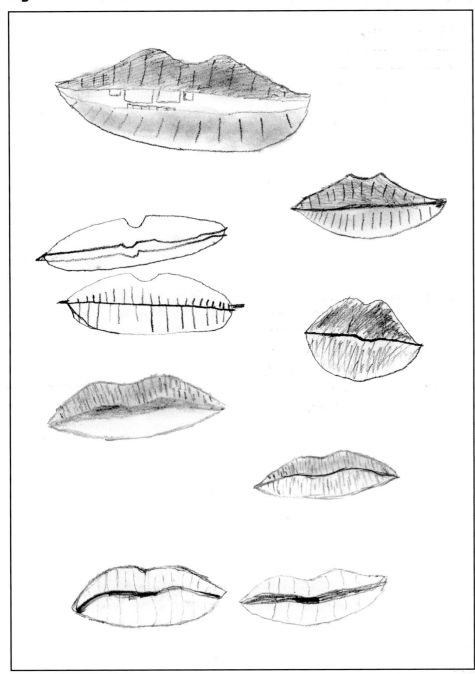

Mouths drawn by Year 6 children

 SKILL

Drawing mouths and noses

Time	Resources	National Curriculum
30 min. approx.	Sketchbooks B or 2B pencils Mirrors	1a, 1b, 2b, 5a

Introduction
'You have worked on drawing heads and the position of the features and have spent some time looking at and drawing eyes. Now you are going to draw noses and mouths. You will be using mirrors to draw your own features and will be looking at each other again.'

Practical activity
Mouths
- ❐ Children look in the mirror and talk about the shape of their mouths.
- ❐ Explain that mouth shapes vary enormously. There are different thicknesses and different widths as well as different shapes.
- ❐ Notice that the distance between the top lip and the base of the nose varies considerably.
- ❐ At this point they could look at their partner's mouth shape and compare it with their own.
- ❐ Mouths can be quite difficult to get right, so remind children to use light lines so they can alter anything they need to. It is probably easier to draw the mouth closed.
- ❐ As the line between the lips is usually the darkest, suggest children draw this first. This is rarely a straight line. Point out that lips have curved vertical lines across them, rather like the segments of worms.
- ❐ Now shade in the upper lip, which is usually more in shadow than the lower.
- ❐ Children could try drawing an open mouth. Ask them to look to see if both upper and lower teeth are visible, or neither. If teeth can be seen they are usually slightly in shadow with much darker shadows behind them.
- ❐ Finally children could shade in the little hollow between the upper lip and the nose.

Noses

- ❏ Noses are quite difficult and also vary enormously in shape and length.
- ❏ Suggest drawing the shape of the nostrils and the shadows inside first.
- ❏ Then draw the shadows on either side of the bridge rather than a line.

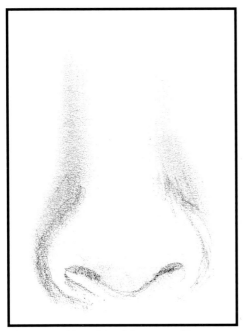

Smudges either side of the nose will create shadows and create the illusion of light along the bridge of the nose.

Background information
Children tend to have developed schema for drawing facial features. This lesson encourages them to have another look at the shapes and to draw what they see rather than what they think they know about them. Profiles are more difficult than full-face portraits, and are briefly covered on pages 130–131.

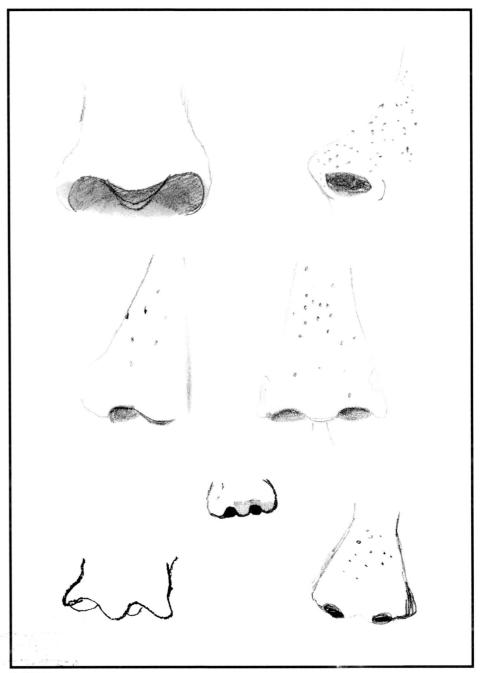

Noses drawn by Year 5 children

Michael Grimshire, Year 5

USING SKILL

Drawing faces

Time:	Resources	National
45–60 min.	Sketchbooks	Curriculum
	B or 2B pencils	1a, 4a, 5a
	Mirrors	
	Resource sheet 26 (page 178)	

Introduction

'Today you are going to draw self-portraits. You will have nearly an hour, which will give you plenty of time to include a lot of detail and shading. You could use the guidelines to check your progress and remember if you use light lines you can change things as you go along if you want to.'

Practical activity

❏ Revise the aspects of portraits that the children have covered so far: head shape, the position and shape of features.

❏ They should start by lightly drawing an oval, nearly filling the paper.

❏ Then draw the neck, noting width, and how it curves out at the base.

❏ Divide the face as illustrated on Resource sheet 26. This will give a framework for the features.

❏ Children should now look in the mirror, at the shape of their faces, altering the oval to match more closely to their own face shape.

❏ Next draw the features, with continual reference to the mirror.

❏ Once the main features are in place, children should add tone.

❏ Point out shaded areas: eye sockets, sides of the nose, underside of chin, also small vertical shadow above top lip. Half closing eyes will help children see the light and dark areas.

❏ Before adding the hair: look to see where it grows from, how far down the face it comes, if it covers the neck, if it is wavy or straight, what tone it is, if the ears are visible. Hair often follows the shape of the head so use line, tone or texture to depict this.

❏ Lastly they could add details: freckles, moles, earrings, collars, etc.

Background information
This lesson is an opportunity for the children to apply all that they have learned about drawing the position and shape of features. They should aim to create a likeness, remembering to use tone, texture and detail.

Children could have copies of the guidelines governing the positions and shapes so they can refer to them if necessary. If they understand that artists change and modify their work all the time, it might help them not to be disheartened when they feel their drawings are not going as well as they would like.

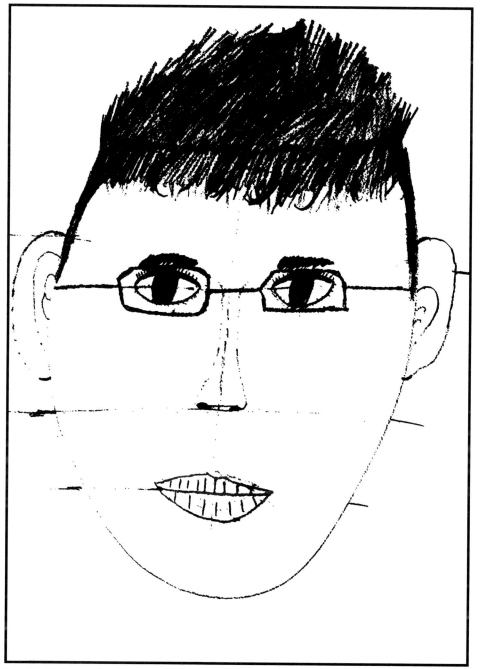

Year 6 child's drawing (see colour illustration on front cover)

129

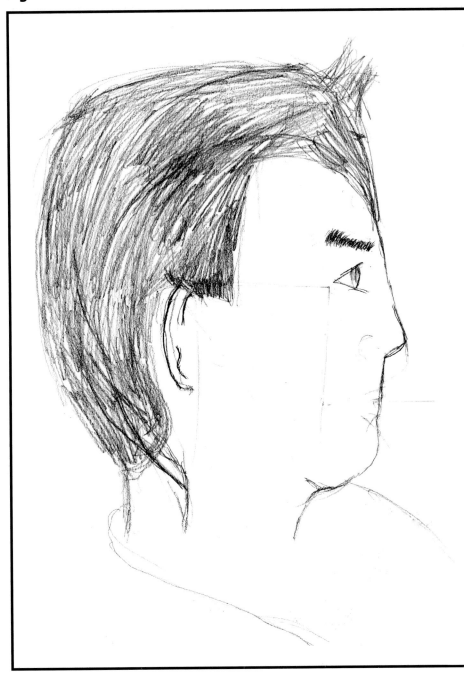

Callum Clark, Year 6

USING
SKILL

Drawing faces in profile
For Year 6 or more able Year 5

Time	Resources	National
45–50 min.	Sketchbooks B or 2B pencils Enlarged copy of Resource sheet 27 (page 179) to model and one per child Model of a skull if you have one, or picture of one	**Curriculum** 1a, 1b, 5a

Introduction
'Drawing a portrait picture from the side is called drawing a profile. The same rules of proportion apply as with full-face portraits, eyes are half-way down the face, ear tips are level with eyebrows, etc. However, because you are seeing the face from a different angle, many shapes look different.'

Practical activity
❏ Remind the children to use light lines to begin with!
❏ Children could take it in turns to pose for each other.
❏ Encourage children to see the overall shape of the head, and the back of the head. They could feel their own head, and how it curves out above the neck.
❏ Now draw the head shape, thinking of the back of the skull under the hair.
❏ Next draw a horizontal line dividing the head in half (excluding neck); the eye will be along this line.
❏ Draw the eye, noting how it is quite a different shape viewed from the side.
❏ Next sub-divide the lower half of the face, as in the diagram. They will now have a frame for the features.
❏ The neck should be added now, noting its backward slanting angle.
❏ The really tricky job is placing the ear (it would help if the model tucks hair behind the ear). Children tend to draw the ears too close to the features.

❒ The area of the cheek could be visualized as a right-angled triangle. The three sides of this are:

1. *From the outer corner of the eye vertically down, passing the corner of the mouth, down to the jaw line.*

2. *From the jaw line diagonally up to the front of the ear, at the place where the ear is widest.*

3. *From the front of the ear horizontally across to the outer corner of the eye.*

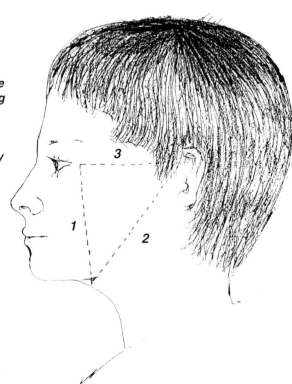

❒ It would be more useful for the children to do several quick sketches of profiles, rather than a detailed study, when first tackling profiles.

Background information
Profile portraits are much more challenging than full-face portraits. One reason is that there are fewer points on the side of a face to use as comparative measuring places. There is a large shape between the side of the nose and the ear. It is this expanse of cheek that is often reduced in drawings. The other problem area is the back of the skull, which curves out above the neck. This is often flattened. Children might find it helpful to compare a skull and some profiles.

Thomas Ellis, Year 5

Left: Eliza Burt, Year 5; middle: Sarah Vanstone, Year 5; right: artist not known (see also illustration on front cover)

 USING SKILL

Detailed whole-body portrait
Longer pose

Time	Resources	National
50–60 min.	Sketchbooks	Curriculum
	Any B pencils (B–4B)	1a, 1b, 3a, 3b,
	Resource sheet 25 (page 177)	5a
	Someone to pose (not a pupil and preferably not the teacher)	

Introduction

'Today you are going to do a figure drawing. You will have at least 45 minutes, excluding the model's breaks, to draw the whole figure. That means you will have plenty of time to check the proportions of the figure and make any necessary changes before you add any details. The finished drawing should include tone, texture and any patterns and details you see.'

Practical activity

❑ Set up a relaxed comfortable pose that a model can hold for 8–10 minutes at a time. If the model is seated they could be reading, but draw children's attention to any foreshortening.

❑ Revise guidelines for body proportions and the system for mapping them out, covered in 'Drawing the whole body' (pages 116–117).

❑ Suggest that they initially try to see the figure as a whole shape, and plan how it will fit on the paper.

❑ When the framework is mapped out, children should do a light drawing of the figure, starting with the head. Discourage any drawing of features, hair or detail at this stage.

❑ Once children are satisfied that the proportions are fairly accurate they can go ahead and add the features and hair.

❑ Now draw attention to folds in clothing, tones, textures and patterns.

❑ Success criteria could be a likeness to the sitter, including distinguishing characteristics, and fairly accurate proportions.

❑ Children should consider their success against these, and think about how they could improve their drawing next time.

Harmony Wilton, Year 5

Chalk and charcoal

Sam Jeffrey, Year 6

133

Rationale

Chalk and charcoal are excellent drawing media as they encourage children to think about a whole subject and not to become lost in detail, as they can often do. For example, they will carefully draw eyelashes when they have not yet drawn the whole figure; they will start to draw patterns on clothing before they have checked body proportions.

Chalk and charcoal encourage them to think big, to concentrate on main features and to think about lights and darks from the moment they put their first marks on paper.

Drawing with chalk and charcoal will help them to get into the habit of seeing and thinking in tones, rather than detail and colour. It can be free, messy and dramatic, or controlled, delicate and subtle. It is also relatively easy to create pleasing pictures and so helps to boost confidence and self-esteem.

Chalk and charcoal are classic drawing media. Across the ages artists have used these drawing materials, for example Rembrandt, Whistler and the contemporary American artist Jim Dine.

Media knowledge

Charcoal is made by sophisticated methods nowadays, but it is basically just burnt wood and is the oldest drawing medium. It has been in use since early cave people covered the walls of their caves with drawings of the animals they hunted, using burnt sticks from their fires and charred bones. It has been made for centuries by the controlled and partial burning of wood. It makes bold black marks, which can be smudged, blended and lightened in different ways.

Chalk is often used with charcoal as a way of picking out highlights and for mixing with charcoal to create mid tones. Adding chalk highlights can bring a charcoal drawing to life, giving it contrast and sparkle.

Different types of charcoal
Stick charcoal
The most common types of charcoal are vine and willow charcoal, which are made in different thicknesses and with different degrees of hardness. Medium thickness is the most versatile, although the fine is useful for more delicate work and the thick for drawings covering large areas or dense coverage. Children tend to worry about charcoal breaking so it is a good idea to snap it into 4 cm lengths in advance.

Charcoal pencils
These are a less messy way of using charcoal as the children's fingers hold the wooden shaft not the actual charcoal, and broken pieces are not forever dropping on the floor. However, they need constant sharpening so can be more trouble than they are worth.

Compressed charcoal
These small sticks are made from powdered charcoal compressed with a binding material. They do not break as easily as stick charcoal but they are less easy to dust off.

Chalk

Ordinary blackboard chalk is perfectly adequate. White chalk pastels or Conté crayons (soft pastels) could also be used.

Fixing drawings

All soft media like chalk and charcoal need 'fixing' as these materials are so soft they will continue to smudge and fade if not fixed when the drawing is finished. Special fixative can be purchased from art suppliers but cheap unscented hairspray makes an acceptable alternative. The drawings should be sprayed when children are out of the room.

Harriet Gregory, Year 5

Tips and techniques

To avoid smudging during drawing

One of the characteristics of chalk and charcoal is that they smudge. Drawings can be spoiled by being leaned on as work progresses so provide the children with pieces of scrap paper to lay between their hands and their drawing. Their hands will rest on this and not on their drawing.

Papers

Chalk and charcoal work looks best on mid-tone tinted sugar paper such as grey, buff or brown. Charcoal is sympathetic to the texture of paper allowing the grain to show through, so paper with a slight roughness to it is ideal. Very smooth or shiny paper should be avoided as the charcoal will slide on the surface and lose its density.

Blending

To create an expanse of blended tone, first build up an area of scribbled marks, pressing evenly but not too heavily. Use the tip of a finger or cotton bud to lightly rub the surface to blend the marks together. The finished effect is a soft, deep shadow which can be drawn over or made deeper by repeating the process. Chalk and charcoal can be blended in the same way.

Lightening

Charcoal can be lifted or lightened in different ways: a soft eraser, pieces of cloth, tissues or even pellets of soft bread. If erasers are being used they need to be as soft as possible, and kept just for use with charcoal, as cleaning them afterwards will take time. Some old erasers could be cut into quarters, as children do not need a whole eraser each.

Charcoal wash

A brush dipped in water applied to parts or the whole of a charcoal drawing creates a grey wash. The tones of the wash soften the fierceness of the black lines and when the wash is dry it can be drawn over, creating a layered effect.

Keeping clean

Children should cover their clothes and roll up or push back their sleeves. They can become agitated at the state of their hands during a charcoal lesson. Explain that some aspects of art are messy and that's the way it is. Discourage washing hands during the lesson; they should just dust their hands together to get the worst off, and carry on.

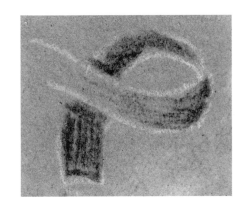

Year 5 children's drawings using charcoal on a mid-tone paper

About this chapter

Children can create dramatic and subtle effects using chalk and charcoal.

They are ideal media for capturing spectacular or dramatic scenes; for example urban landscapes, bare winter trees, a sudden fall of snow, or a stormy sky with lashing rain. They can be equally effective when depicting delicate subjects such as feathers or shells.

Chalk and charcoal can also be used to great effect in portrait work. The chalk highlights 'lift' the drawings, giving them a sparkle and crispness. Children are often delighted with the results.

In this chapter children will experiment with making marks with chalk and charcoal.

They will blend and smudge them together and use chalk to create highlights. They will use erasers to lift areas of charcoal and create lighter tones.

They will look carefully to identify the darkest and lightest tones in their subject and try to recreate these in chalk, charcoal or a blend of the two.

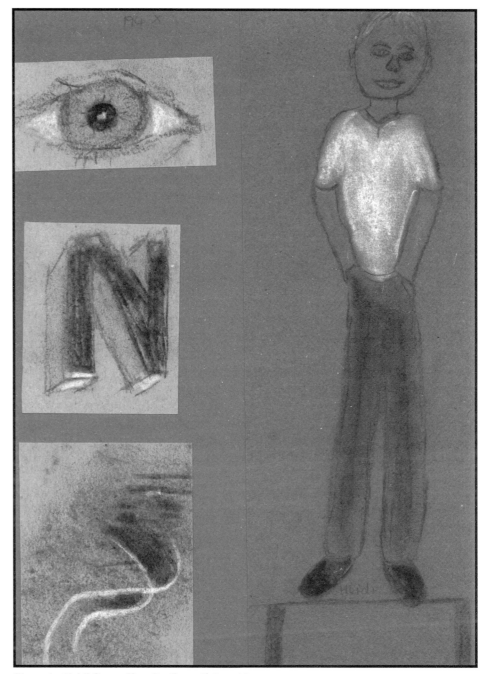

Figure by Heidi Green, Year 6; other artists not known

A year 5 child's collection of marks in chalk and charcoal on a mid-tone paper

 KEY SKILL

Making different marks in chalk and charcoal

Time	Resources	National
15–20 min.	Mid-tone sugar paper (any colour, but grey or brown look good) Charcoal, two different thicknesses if possible, broken into 4 cm pieces White chalks or white soft chalky pastels Some old erasers Fixative (see Glossary) Scrap paper	Curriculum 2a, 2b, 4a

Introduction

'Charcoal is made of specially burnt wood; it has been a drawing medium since the days of the cave people. It makes dramatic dark marks, smudges and is ideal for quick bold drawings. Chalk used with charcoal makes effective contrasts; touches of chalk can bring a drawing to life. Today you are going to investigate the different effects you can make in chalk and charcoal. Charcoal blends well with chalk to make medium tones; chalk can also be used for highlights. You can also make highlights by removing areas of tone with an eraser.'

Practical activity

☐ Children experiment with charcoal to produce as many different tones as possible, using the point of the charcoal and then the side.

☐ Tell them to blend some marks by smudging, and to see if they can phase out the tone so it becomes almost invisible.

☐ Next, children chalk over some of their charcoal markings and blend them together with a finger.

☐ They could draw a circle in charcoal and then gradually shade in, lightening the tone as they get nearer the middle, adding chalk highlights in the centre. It should now look three-dimensional.

❑ Children can experiment with patches of chalk and charcoal in different degrees of tone, enclosing light circles in darker areas and dark squares inside lighter areas.

❑ They could try lifting areas of tone with erasers, and adding dark backgrounds behind shaded cubes and spheres.

A year 6 child's experimentation in creating the illusion of three dimensions, using chalk and charcoal on a mid-tone paper

Drawing with chalk and charcoal

Time	Resources	National
30–45 min.	Mid-tone sugar paper (at least A4)	Curriculum
	Charcoal, broken into 4 cm pieces	1a, 1c, 2a, 4a,
	White chalk	5a
	Old erasers	
	Scrap paper if working indoors	
	Fixative (see Glossary)	

Introduction

'You have been investigating different effects you can make with chalk and charcoal. Now you are going to have the opportunity to use these effects in your drawings.'

Practical activity

❒ Children draw a quick light outline of their subject in chalk, with no detail.

❒ Next ask them to tell you where the darkest areas are. (They could try half closing their eyes to get an overall image; sometimes it is easier to see the main tonal contrasts this way.)

❒ These should now be blocked in.

❒ Children now build up the rest of the picture in different tones, some charcoal and some blended chalk and charcoal, wherever appropriate.

❒ Remind them that smudging creates different effects.

❒ Children can create highlights with chalk, and by lifting areas of charcoal using an old eraser. Line, pattern or texture detail could be added on top later.

Background information

There are many subjects that are suitable for drawing in chalk and charcoal. Portraits are ideal for indoor subjects; choose the model carefully to ensure they are wearing a range of tones with some white. The white helps give the drawing contrast. Large flowering plants can look good drawn in this medium. The best subjects are to be found outdoors. School buildings have strong shapes, shadows and highlights on windows. A dark tree silhouetted against a mid-tone sky with light clouds is another good subject. Snow scenes can look stunning. Encourage the children to work quickly and be bold.

Snap the charcoal into short lengths (4 cm) so children can draw with the side and the point.

In order that drawings are not spoiled by being smudged as work progresses, provide the children with a piece of scrap paper that can be laid over any completed sections of their work. Drawings can be sprayed with fixative later, when children have left the room.

Leanna Lyons-Martin, Year 5

Becky Jewel, Year 6

Evaluation and assessment

Assessment

Children need to reflect on their artwork and should share in assessment where appropriate. They should be clear which aspect of their artwork is being assessed, and what they need to do to meet the assessment criteria.

Realistically, drawing needs only to be assessed in broad terms: identify those children who are struggling and will need to cover the work again or in a different way, and those children who have excelled and could be stretched.

One way might be to broadly group pupils into three ability bands. At the end of a term, chapter or whenever appropriate, select a small number of pupils from each band and assess their work. From this make a general assumption that other pupils in the same band will have achieved a similar standard. At the end of the next term or chapter, select a different group of pupils so that over the course of a term (or a year) all pupils will have been assessed.

Another way to make the assessment process easier is to photocopy the class list and attach it to the drawing skills assessment sheet (Resource sheet 28, page 180). Highlight the aspect(s) you are going to assess. (Limit this to a maximum of three, unless this is an end of year assessment.) Then, using a colour code (e.g. green for excellent, yellow for satisfactory and red for problems), highlight the children's names with the appropriate colours on the class list. Further comments could be added if necessary. An example assessment record is given on this page.

Drawing assessments

Class:

Date:

Colour code
Green = Excellent
Yellow = Satisfactory
Red = Needs further help

1. Uses a variety of lines in drawings
2. Uses tone in drawings
3. Identifies areas for development in own drawings

	1	2	3
John Brown			
Priya Gil			
Mary Green			
An Other			

Example of assessment record

Evaluation and assessment

Assessment should inform planning. If the majority of the class have not met the success criteria, the task needs to be re-evaluated.

Try to be specific when making your judgements:

❐ Was it too hard?
❐ Was the explanation clear enough?
❐ Does it need to be done again in the same way or differently?
❐ Which elements of my teaching do I need to change?
❐ When and how will this be done in the same way or differently?

Figure and face drawings could be assessed against the shapes and proportions guidelines found on pages 114–115 and Resource sheets 25 and 26 (pages 177 and 178).

Older or more able children could check their own drawings, write comments on their achievements and give themselves targets, as in this example:

'I am pleased with my portrait. I think I managed to get the proportions about right. I think the head is too big. I found out when I counted how many went into the body. Next time I will try to remember not to do too much detail before I check the proportions.'

Jack, age 10

It is as well to support them with their targets, otherwise they tend to be vague or nearly impossible. For example, *'I want to get better at drawing,'* or *'I want to be able to draw the final battle in the Lord of the Rings.'*

Using success criteria to evaluate children's work

Work can also be evaluated against success criteria based on the aspects of the chapter that are going to be assessed. Success criteria should really be drawn up with the pupils as the direct teaching or explanation is taking place. For example, after the skill has been taught but before it is going to be used in a context, say, *'We have been learning how to make our drawings more interesting by using lots of different lines. I want you to remember to use as many of the different kinds of lines as you think will be right for the job in your drawings today* (run over the variety of lines covered). *I shall be looking at your drawings to see if you have used a range of lines.'*

Use a 'must, should, could' system of success criteria. For example, for a Year 5–6 lesson on line work in pencil, write up on the board:

Success criteria
1. You **must** use a good variety of different lines.
2. You **should** use both the side and the point of the pencil.
3. You **could** use lines to create a dramatic or subtle effect.

Work can then be judged against these criteria. Four criteria are really the maximum, the fourth being useful for stretching more able pupils.

Success criteria are also useful for children's self-assessment.

There are success criteria for using line in pencil drawings on page 22 in the chapter on Line.

Self-evaluation

In order to evaluate their work, children need to be given the vocabulary necessary to do this and possibly also a framework.

Internal self-evaluation

During the drawing process, a constant internal evaluation should be taking place. Examples of this kind of internal dialogue are given on page 95.

Further self-questioning might include:
- ❐ How is this going?
- ❐ Am I pleased with it?
- ❐ What should I change?
- ❐ How am I going to change it?
- ❐ Is it finished?
- ❐ What is good / not so good about it?
- ❐ How does it look if I hold it away from myself a little?
- ❐ How would it look to someone else?
- ❐ How does it look on the paper?
- ❐ Have I placed it on the paper well?

Spoken self-evaluation

Internal self-evaluation naturally leads on to being able to review what they have done and say what they think and feel about it.

Here the vocabulary may need to be modelled by teacher questioning.

The following questions could be asked:
- ❐ What are you most pleased about with this piece of work?
- ❐ What part do you think is most successful? (the composition, the use of media, the tones, textures, patterns, shapes)
- ❐ What did you find most difficult?
- ❐ What problems did you meet?
- ❐ How did you solve / not solve those problems?
- ❐ If you did it again is there anything you would change?
- ❐ How would you change it?
- ❐ If you had more time what would you do next?
- ❐ Are you proud of it?
- ❐ Would it look very different / better if you ... used different paper / media / changed the scale / looked at it from a distance / changed the colours?

Developing this kind of questioning will help children talk about their work and be able to make internal independent judgements as they mature.

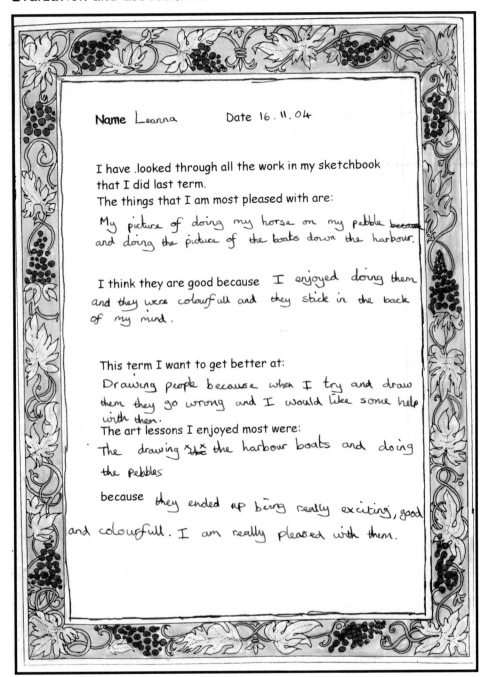

Name Leanna   Date 16.11.04

I have looked through all the work in my sketchbook
that I did last term.
The things that I am most pleased with are:

My picture of doing my horse on my pebble because
and doing the picture of the boats down the harbour.

I think they are good because I enjoyed doing them
and they were colourfull and they stick in the back
of my mind.

This term I want to get better at:
Drawing people because when I try and draw
them they go wrong and I would like some help
with them.
The art lessons I enjoyed most were:
The drawing of the harbour boats and doing
the pebbles

because they ended up being really exciting, good
and colourfull. I am really pleased with them.

Examples of Resource sheet 29 completed by Leanna Lyons-Martin, Year 5

Written evaluations

Written evaluations can take different forms.

Children could annotate their work on the border or underneath, especially in their sketchbooks. Language is as for spoken self-evaluations. For example:

> *'I am really pleased with this. I think I made the house look three-dimensional, but I think the trees are too small.'*

Children could use Resource sheet 29 (page 181) – see the example on this page. These are very useful at the end of a chapter, term or year. They can be pasted into sketchbooks and referred to at a later date. For example, *'Remember what you said you wanted to get better at this term. Look back in your sketchbooks and remind yourself of what you wrote.'* Children could also include a personal target, e.g. *'Next term I want to get better at ...'*

The same kind of language can be used when writing comments in sketchbooks. For example, *'This is a careful, sensitive drawing. Were you pleased with it? Which part were you most pleased with?'* Or, *'I can see you had problems with this. What did you find most difficult? How would you do it differently if you did it again?'*

Children could be encouraged to look for teacher comments and questions in their sketchbooks and write a response if appropriate. They could also be encouraged to periodically look back through their sketchbooks to see if they think they are making progress, and write comments against their favourite piece of work. For example: *'I am really proud of this because ... '.*

Resource sheet 28 (page 180) provides a comprehensive drawing skills assessment list for individual children.

Peer evaluation

Children should be able to review the artwork of their peers and say what they think and feel about it. The same kind of language can be used for this as for self-evaluation. Children, however, need to learn to be sensitive to each other and to be 'critical friends'. They need to be able to trust each other and be thoughtful and supportive in their comments. In the early stages of developing peer evaluation they need to be confined to positive comments. Later, when trust has been built up and children are better able to express their responses using appropriate vocabulary, some supportive criticism can be introduced. Again this will need to be modelled. For example:

❐ What do you think Emma could do to this drawing to make it even better?

❐ What problems do you think Dan had with this drawing? How could he solve it?

The peer evaluation can be built into the lesson, and then used in the plenary or summing up at the end of the session. At appropriate points during the drawing lesson, ask children to stop drawing and take a walk around the classroom and have a look at each other's drawings. Tell them to do this in silence with no spoken comments.

Ask them to look at each other's drawings and ask themselves questions like:

❐ Is it good? What is good about it?

❐ Is it not so good? What has gone wrong?

❐ How should it be put right?

❐ If it was your drawing what would you do next?

❐ Are there any good ideas (not copying) you could use in your drawing?

Explain to them that artists get inspiration from other artists. Artists will often talk to each other about their work and the ideas that are generated will often be crucial to the artist's development.

At the end of the lesson one child could be asked to select another pupil's piece of work to comment on. This could be modelled. For example:

❐ Why do you like this drawing?

❐ What do you think Jade has done particularly well?

❐ How do you think she has achieved that effect?

❐ Did she remember all the things she was supposed to (relating to the focus of the lesson)?

Then Jade could be asked:

❐ Are you pleased with it?

❐ If so, why? What were you most pleased with?

❐ Would you change anything if you had time?

❐ How would you do it differently next time?

She in turn could be asked to choose another child's work to talk about.

Potential pitfall!
Children often choose their best friend's work to make positive comments about. Pre-empt this by saying you will be asking them to give precise reasons why they think their chosen drawing is good.

Reporting and tracking progress

One way to keep track of progress is to collect sample drawings from the whole class biannually or termly. These can be annotated and kept in a file. Over a number of years this will give a record of each child's drawing development over their time in school.

Children's drawings tell a lot about children's maturity and something of their character.

The filed drawings are useful for planning and for reporting to parents and showing to Ofsted as evidence of progression.

The drawings must be collected in the same way each time and in the same circumstances. For example, children should be allocated the same time for each sample drawing (e.g. 10 minutes), are given the same medium (e.g. pencil), and the same subject matter (e.g. figure drawing), it will then be easier to compare drawings.

Drawings can be compared against the previous term's drawings and against the general standard of the year group.

Another way would be to take a sample of a figure drawing one term, a landscape the next term and a close observational drawing from the last term. These drawings can be annotated, with specific strengths or weaknesses noted and possible ways forward. The class teacher or the art co-ordinator could keep the files.

Recording coverage of work

To check coverage of chapters, photocopy the relevant part of the contents list. Highlight the lessons covered, possibly making a written note beside the lesson of the programmes of study covered. These are to be found in the box at the top of the lesson pages. The skills in this book cover all the programmes of study relating to drawing, evaluating and developing work.

A colour code could be used: green for covered satisfactorily, and red for lessons that were not successful for some reason. A note could be made by these for future reference.

To check for National Curriculum coverage, photocopy the programmes of study for the appropriate year group and highlight the ones that have been covered.

Both these records of coverage could be kept in a planning or records file.

If you are using the QCA schemes of work, the skills required could be taught prior to delivering the QCA unit. Some QCA units cover a fair amount of portrait work, such as Unit 6a, People in Action. Other units which involve observational drawing would benefit from having drawing and looking skills taught prior to the delivery of the unit.

Reports

Here are some statements which might be useful when writing reports:

- ❐ Has acquired / is acquiring drawing skills after working in a range of media
- ❐ Draws well / is beginning to draw with great sensitivity to line and tone
- ❐ Has developed / is beginning an understanding of pattern/tone/texture
- ❐ Demonstrates good drawing skills in all designing activities
- ❐ Is able to draw and talk about familiar objects
- ❐ Is able to talk about own work using appropriate vocabulary
- ❐ Is able to discuss own work and say what he / she might change or develop in the future
- ❐ Is developing good powers of observation
- ❐ Shows close attention to detail when drawing.

Less positive comments:
- ❐ Finds some aspects of this subject difficult but is working hard to improve skills
- ❐ Needs to be more willing to discuss a piece of work and how it might be improved
- ❐ Must avoid the tendency to rush, and spend a little more time looking and thinking carefully when drawing.

Zac Anderson, Year 6

Glossary

Art pastels: Soft chalky pastels, quite smudgy.

Bleed/move: A term which describes what happens when a colour runs when wet or wetted.

Brusho: Powdered watercolour that can be sprinkled directly onto wet drawings, or made up with water as a thin paint. Usually comes in lovely bright colours but can be used for delicate or translucent colour.

Cartridge paper: Slightly rough paper of medium weight, ideal for drawing and painting, can be coloured.

Charcoal: Specially burnt twigs used for drawing, comes in different thicknesses. Drawings usually need fixing, with fixative or hairspray.

Composition: The arrangement of elements in a picture.

Conté crayons (soft pastels): Drawing medium made from compressed coloured chalk, often in earth or landscape colours.

Contour: The edge as seen around the outside of a shape or form.

Cross-hatching: Form of shading created by crossed lines.

Elements: As referred to in the National Curriculum for Art and Design: line, tone, shape, form, pattern, colour, texture and space.

Etching: Type of printing, blocks usually made by acid eating into uncovered parts of metal plate. Plate is then inked and prints are taken.

Fixative: Spray used to prevent charcoal or chalky pastel drawings from further smudging. Can be purpose bought, but cheap unscented hairspray makes a good substitute. Fixative should always be used when children have left the room and will not be back for an hour or so, as some children may be sensitive to the fumes.

Foreground: Lower area of drawing representing the area nearest to viewer.

Form: The three-dimensional shape of something.

Graphite: Hard drawing medium, silvery lead colour.

Landscape: Paper alignment when paper is placed with shorter sides vertical.

Medium/media: Different drawing materials: pencil, charcoal, pen, etc.

Move/bleed: A term which describes what happens when a colour runs when wet or wetted.

Narrative drawing: A drawing which tells a story in some way, or a sequence of events.

Oil pastels: Slightly sticky pastels made from coloured chalk bound with oil. Colours blend well. Useful for creating scraper and wax-resist pictures.

Op Art: Short for optical art, pictures usually consisting of lines or shapes that create optical illusions. Often giving the illusion of movement.

Pattern: An image that is repeated in a regular fashion.

People crayons: Commercially produced crayons, usually sold in a pack, made up of colours for different skin, hair and eyes.

Portrait: Paper alignment when paper is placed with shorter sides horizontal.

Schema: A formulated drawing that children have arrived at which represents, say, a house, a tree or a person, which they then use every time to represent that subject, even when drawing from first-hand experience.

Single-hatching: A series of single lines, drawn close together to create an area of tone.

Surrealism: An art movement which uses realist images but puts them together in an unusual or dream-like way. Salvador Dali is a Surrealist artist.

Texture: In drawing, texture means creating the impression something has a surface feel to it.

Tone: Darkness or lightness of a colour (including gradual shades of black through to white).

Viewfinder: Piece of black card, plastic or paper with a shape cut out of the middle. This is used to look closely at areas of a drawing or artefact. Can be used as a frame, to help children to compose a picture. The centre shape can be round, oval, square, rectangular, to suit purpose.

Bibliography

Barnes, Rob. *Art, Design and Topic Work 8–13*, Routledge Taylor & Francis

Camp, Jeffrey. *Draw: How to Master the Art*, Dorling Kindersley

Capon, Robin. *Drawing Techniques*, The Crowood Press

Clement, Robert, and Page, Shirley. *Primary Art: Investigating and Making in Art* , Oliver & Boyd

Cole, Roger. *Drawing with Children*, Private publication

Cox, Maureen. *Children's Drawing*, Penguin Books

da Vinci, Leonardo et al. *A Treatise on Painting,* Dover Publications

Devon Curriculum Advice. *Planning, Evaluation and Assessment*, DCA

DfEE. *Art and Design National Curriculum*, Qualifications and Curriculum Authority

Dixon, Peter. *Standing Points*, Private publication

Dobson, Bert. *Keys to Drawing*, A&C Black

Edwards, Betty. *Drawing on the Right Side of the Brain*, Harper Collins

Elderfield, John. *The Drawings of Henri Matisse*, W W Norton

Foster, Patience. *Drawing*, Usbourne

Frank, Frederick. *The Zen of Seeing: Seeing Drawing as Meditation*, Random House

Gormley, Antony. *Drawing*, British Museum Press

Hayes, Colin. *The Complete Guide to Painting and Drawing Techniques and Materials*, Phaidon

Lemos, Pedro. *Applied Art*, Pacific Press Publishing Association

Mann, Ida, and Pirie, Antoinette. *The Science of Seeing*, Pelican Books

Mendelowitz, Daniel M. *Drawing: A Study Guide*, Holt Rinehart & Winston

Nicolaides, Kimon. *The Natural Way to Draw*, Andre Deutsch

Parramon, Joe. *The Complete Book of Drawing*, Phaidon

Robinson, Gillian. *Sketchbooks: Explore and Store*, Hodder Arnold

Sedgewick, Dawn and Fred. *Drawing to Learn*, Hodder Arnold

Simpson, Ian. *Drawing, Seeing and Observation*, A&C Black

van Gogh, Vincent. *The Letters* (translated by Arnold Pomerans), Penguin Classics

Welton, Jude. *Drawing: A Young Artist's Guide*, Dorling Kindersley

Williams, Geoffrey. *African Designs*, Dover Publications

Holly Peacock, Year 6 (appears in colour on front cover)

Useful websites

www.aboriginalartonline.com
Australian Aboriginal Dreamtime images and stories.

www.accessart.org.uk
Useful information on drawing and children's interactive art activities.

www.artcyclopedia.com
Excellent access to galleries, museums and artists. Easy to search.

www.arteducation.com
Lesson plans on art topics. Includes step-by-step guidance with teacher's notes.

www.artteaching.co.uk
Has links to art galleries. Click on multicultural art for Aboriginal art, Hindu art, Islamic and Ancient Egyptian art.

www.davidmach.com
Website of British artist David Mach.

www.drawingpower.org.uk
Find out about the national campaign for drawing.

www.drumcroon.org.uk
For anyone interested in promoting education through art. Has links to other galleries.

www.google.co.uk
This is a brilliant search engine for images. Having opened up Google, click on 'images' and type in your request. Shows pages of related images.

www.metmuseum.org
Displays more than 3,500 works from New York's Metropolitan Museum, includes growing timeline of international developments in art.

www.moma.org
New York's monumental gallery of modern art.

www.mos.org/leonardo/index.html
Child-friendly site, easy access, lots of interesting information about Leonardo da Vinci. NB: Note his eyes following the cursor on the opening page!

www.nationalgallery.org.uk
The National Gallery website. Has an education section.

www.npg.org.uk
The National Portrait Gallery. An excellent resource, including an education department.

www.nsead.org
Website of the National Society for Education in Art and Design. Among other useful and up-to-date information about art education, has database of around 300 units of work.

www.tate.org.uk
The Tate gallery's website.

www.vangoghgallery.com
Lists and displays all van Gogh's drawings.

Vincent van Gogh, Thatched Roofs

Vincent van Gogh, A Corner of the Garden of St Paul's Hospital at Rémy, 1889

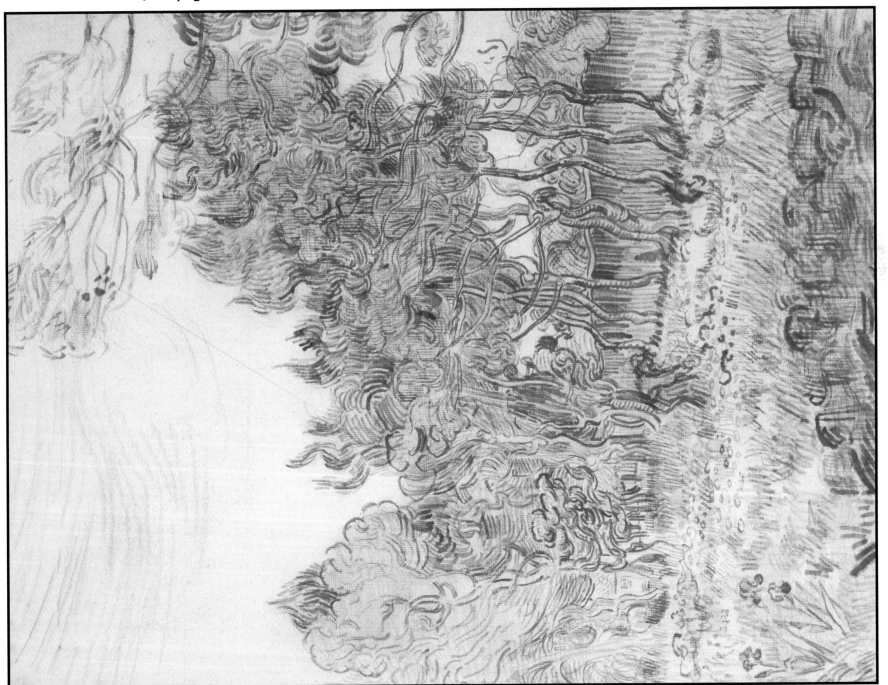

Examples of single-hatching ▼   ▶

'And Who Are You?' by Sir Nathaniel Dance-Holland

'James Leckie and Little Mary' by William Mulready

Example of cross-hatching ▶

'Reaper' (e) by Richard Hamilton © Richard Hamilton 2005. All Rights Reserved, DACS

David Bomberg, *The City on the Rock, Evening, Rhonda, Spain*

Edward Hopper, Study for Manhattan Bridge Loop (No. 2)

Tone record sheet

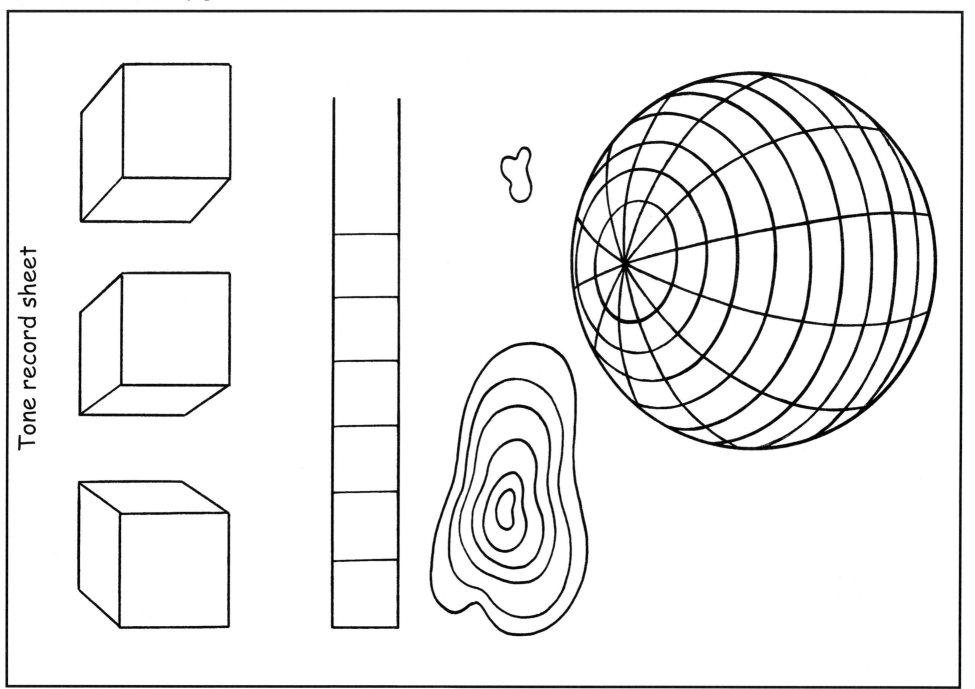

Using tone to shade three-dimensional shapes

Decide which side is going to be furthest away from the light. Shade it in a very dark tone. Leave one side light and shade the third side a medium tone.

Shading wraps around a curved surface. The tone lightens or darkens gradually.

Decide where the light is coming from.

Dark to light to dark.

Dark to lighter to light.

Decide where the light is coming from and shade in these 3-D shapes.

Charcoal record sheet

Light tone

Medium tone

Dark tone

Light single-hatching

Medium single-hatching

Dark single-hatching

Light cross-hatching

Medium cross-hatching

Dark cross-hatching

Light cross-hatching smudged

Medium cross-hatching smudged

Dark cross-hatching smudged

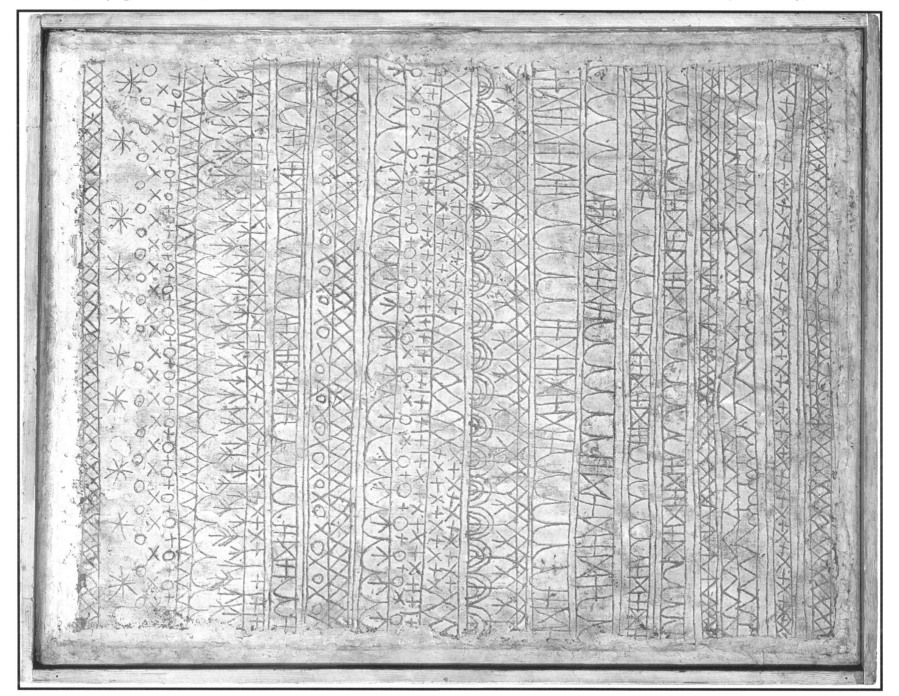

Making doodles

Start with a simple shape.

Add to it. You could use handwriting patterns, dots, single- or cross-hatching.

The doodle should grow slowly.
Draw as carefully as you can.

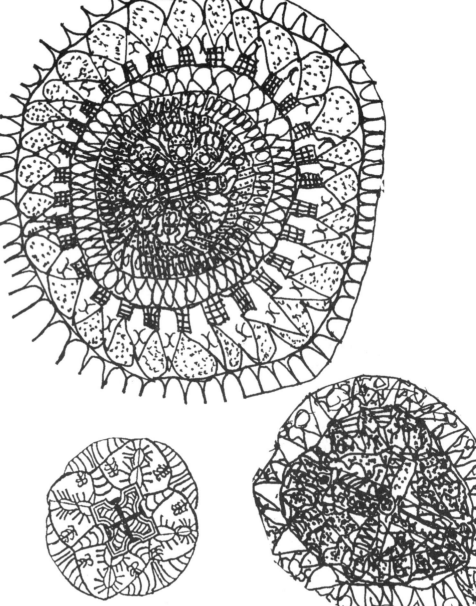

Handwriting patterns

Continue these handwriting patterns.

Marigold ▲

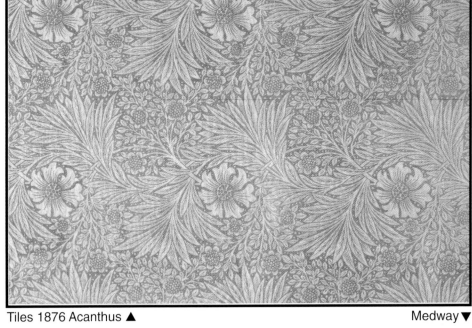

Tiles 1876 Acanthus ▲

Pimpernell ▼

Medway ▼

Different ways to draw cubes and cuboids

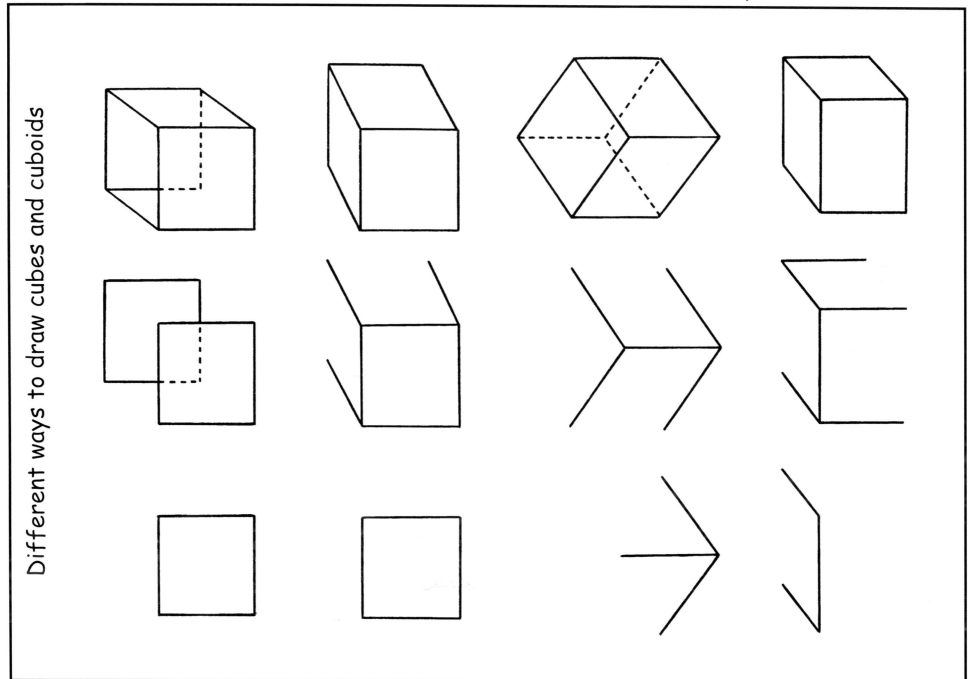

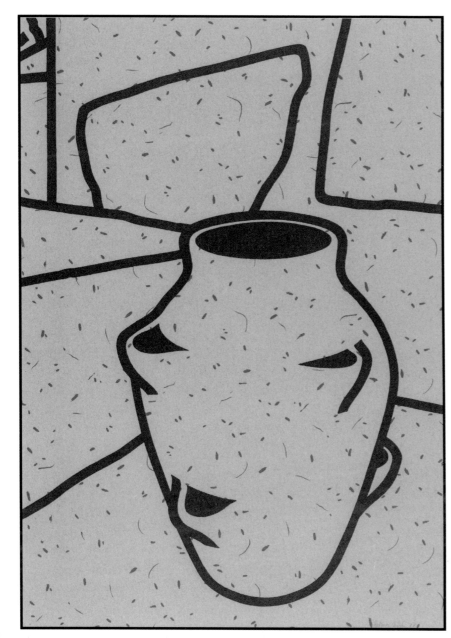

'Plant Pot' by Patrick Caulfield © The Estate of Patrick Caulfield 2005. All Rights
Reserved, DACS

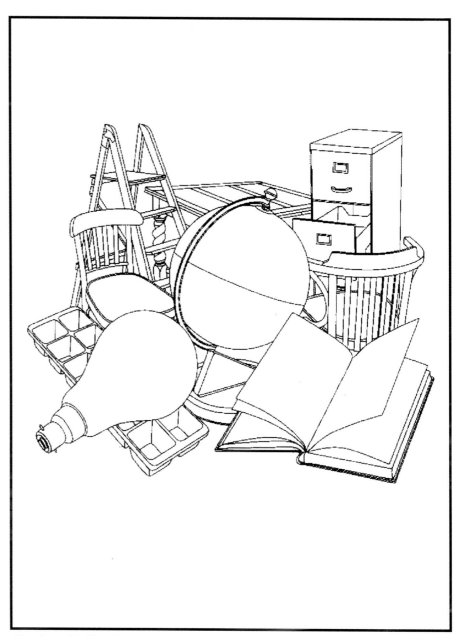

'Reading with Globe' by Micheal Craig-Martin

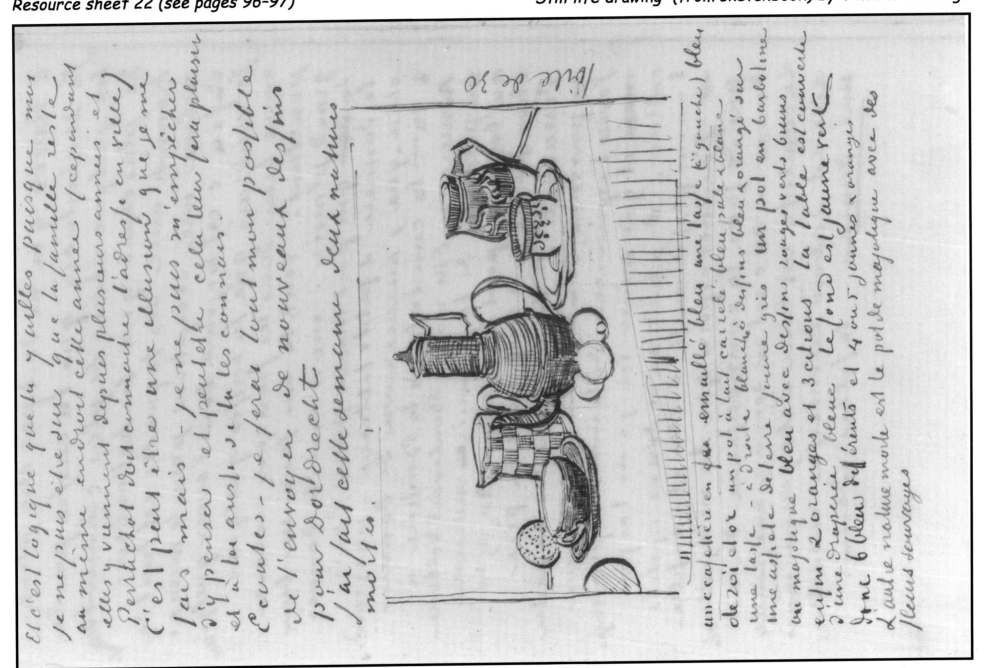

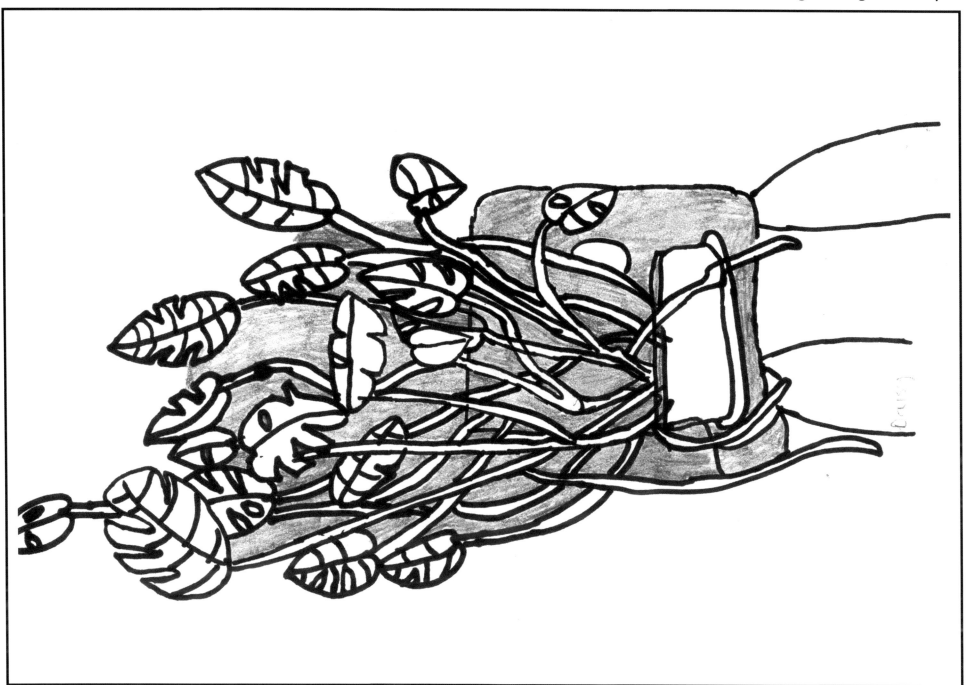

Keep the paper this way up.

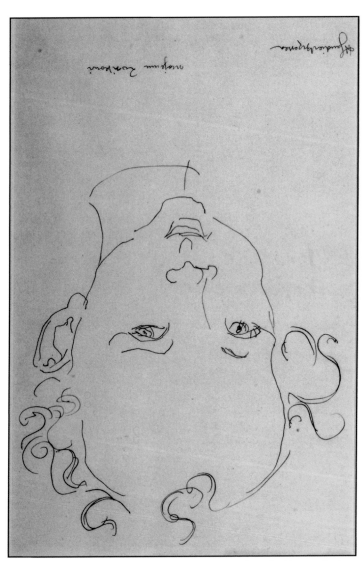

'Head of Child' by Henri Gaudier-Brezska (reproduced with permission

Start drawing from this end.

Guidelines for drawing figures

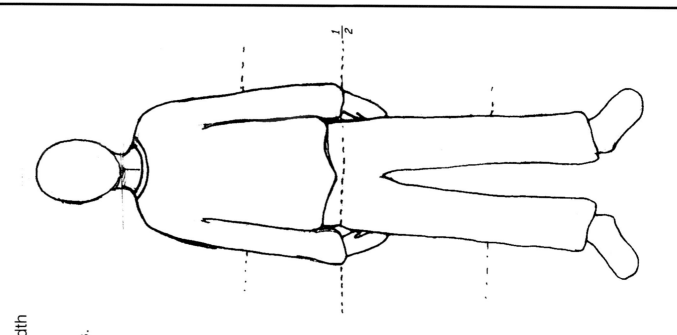

☐ You can fit about 5–6 heads into a child's body (6–7 into an adult's body).

☐ The middle of the body is the hip line (not the waist).

☐ Arms (when hanging down) end half way down the thighs.

☐ The shoulders are at least twice the width of the face.

☐ Necks are slightly narrower than heads.

☐ Foot length is similar to head length.

Guidelines for drawing faces

- [ ] From the front, heads are roughly oval.

- [ ] Faces vary in shape, some are more square, some more pointed, some more rounded.

- [ ] Eyes are almond shaped.

- [ ] Eyelashes grow out of eyelids.

- [ ] Eyes come half way down the face.

- [ ] The pupils are in line with the corners of the mouth.

- [ ] The base of the nose is half way between the eyes and the chin.

- [ ] The mouth is roughly half way between the base of the nose and the chin.

- [ ] You can rarely see the whole iris.

- [ ] The line between the lips is the darkest.

- [ ] Tops of ears are roughly level with eyebrows.

- [ ] Hairline starts below the top of the head (unless the model is balding!).

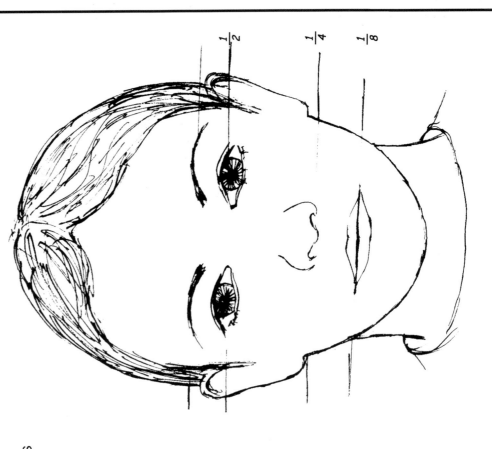

$\dfrac{1}{2}$ $\dfrac{1}{4}$ $\dfrac{1}{8}$